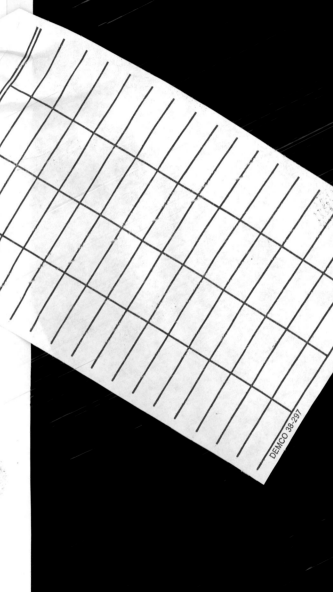

DATE DUE

DEMCO 38-297

Our Modern Times

Our Modern Times

The New Nature of
Capitalism in the
Information Age

Daniel Cohen

translated by Susan Clay and
Daniel Cohen

The MIT Press
Cambridge, Massachusetts
London, England

Set in Palatino by The MIT Press. Printed and bound in the United States of America.

Library of Congress Cataloging-in-Publication Data

Cohen, Daniel, 1953–
[Nos temps modernes. English]
Our modern times : the new nature of capitalism in the information age / Daniel Cohen ; translated by Susan Clay and Daniel Cohen.
p. cm.
Translation of: Nos temps modernes.
Includes bibliographical references and index.
ISBN 0-262-03302-X (hc. : alk. paper)
1. Economics—Sociological aspects. 2. Work—Social aspects. 3. Human capital. I. Title.
HM548 .C6413 2003
306.3—dc21   2002075377

for Pauline, Clara, and Martine

Contents

Our Modern Times

Introduction

Most people have a tendency to see centralized systems in everything. When they see a flock of birds, they think that the front bird is the boss and that the other birds are following it, when actually it's a decentralized system, where simple rules produce complex behaviors, just like fish in a school or cars on a highway.

Do you have a political idea behind this?

It's true that I am motivated in part by social and political reasons. And, in effect, I would have had sympathy for a less hierarchical political system, a society that gave more power to individuals. But one must be careful with that. I'm from the left, but I have been attacked by the left because certain of these ideas can be seen as supporting rightist "laissez-faire" economics. And that puts me ill at ease because I don't want my work to lend any support to this approach to economics of which I don't approve.

These remarks were collected in the course of an interview given to the French newspaper *Libération* by Mitchell Resnik, a professor at the Massachusetts Institute of Technology's famous Media Lab, one of the high circles of the cyber revolution. The discomfort he describes summarizes perfectly the hopes and betrayals of the contemporary world. The new technologies were brought to life by a generation of young people who thought they were criticizing capitalism. As the historian François Caron says, it is "the anti-establishment hedonism of the 1960s that is realized in society's technologization in the 1970s and 1980s."[1] Yet, rather than criticize capitalism, the new technologies gave it a "new spirit," a new breath of life.

This application of the law of unintended consequences is not a surprise. A hundred years earlier, electricity brought the same disappointment to those who trusted that it would break down the "factory system." One witness to this was the French novelist Emile Zola, who after writing *La Bête humaine*, one of the harshest critiques of the industrial age, produced *Le Travail*, a hymn to electricity. Electricity was indeed expected to rescue the bulk of the small workshops that still dominated industrial production. These workshops, with no energy source of their own, faced competition from "large establishments" fortunate enough to have steam engines at their disposal. Contrary to the expectations of the smaller facilities, electricity would only betray their hope. By rendering the production process easier to regulate and to parcel, electricity gave birth to the "Taylorist" assembly line and to "very" large establishments, thus becoming a party to the downfall of the small shops.

The simple reason why it appears so hard to foresee the impact of new technologies is that they are not in themselves the full story. Electricity says little in itself about the kind of capitalism that it may generate. One cannot grasp the full significance of a new technology without understanding how it gets to interact with the organization of labor and without understanding the consumer society it feeds.

You may miss the story of the impact of technologies if you don't open the black box of production and consumption. On the production side, for instance, economists have long been amazed by the "Solow paradox," according to which one sees computers everywhere but in the data on workers' productivity. As Philippe Askenazy demonstrated in a brilliant 1999 thesis,[2] this paradox is readily explained when account is taken of the organization of labor: firms that used computers but did not reorganize their work practices appeared to experience a fall in their total productivity, while firms that reorganized their work practices experienced a steep increase in productivity almost immediately.

In order to grasp the significance of these new work relationships and their link to the new technologies, it is useful to sketch briefly the mechanism that brought the old "Taylorist" organization of labor to an end. One can distinguish two different logics, one of which can be called internal and one of which is external to the organization of labor itself. The internal logic that brought the demise of the old organization of labor is apparent from its very beginning. Workers who are asked to repeat indefinitely the same task all day long are rapidly bored. Lack of attention and absenteeism rapidly plagued the "scientific" organization of labor. As early as in 1914, Henry Ford understood that he needed to do something to raise the morale of his troops. In one of the most famous episodes of labor relations, he decided to double their wages up to the famous five dollars a day per worker. This incentive, which is known in the literature as the "efficiency wage," has a limit, however. What matters in keeping a worker on the job is not that he should be paid more than before but that he should be paid more than he would earn in another job. As the Fordist methods spread to the entire economy, wages pressures were bound to end up as inflation and/or unemployment. In the early 1960s, when the Japanese first attempted to build a car industry of their own, they rapidly understood the internal limits of the Fordist model. This is what brought them to invent a new work practice that gave the worker more autonomy and more responsibility. (It came to be known as "Toyotaism.") In the language of the "efficiency wage" model, however, this merely amounted to changing the monitoring devices used to keep the workforce focused on its tasks.

However, another external force has also been at work. When Ford designed the assembly line model, his main objective was to make the mass of illiterate workers who were looking for jobs—many of them immigrants who had come to the United States at the beginning of the twentieth century—productive. Ford liked to say that he did not expect his workers to read or speak English; he just expected them not to drink on the job. Yet over the course of the century the children of these workers did learn to read and speak English. The tension between an organization of labor that remained essentially unchanged until the 1960s and the baby boomers then entering the labor market became explosive. All over the industrialized world, May 1968 marked the rejection by the newcomers of a work world of hierarchies and obedience—a world that was not designed for them.

It is the encounter between these two forces—a new work practice coming from Japan (ironically, a highly hierarchical society) and a new technological model aimed at eliminating the power of hierarchies over the baby boomer generation that characterizes our contemporary modern times. Its logic is almost opposite to the old one. Workers are asked to be autonomous, to use their "human capital," and this should constitute progress with respect to the assembly line age when people were treated as automatons. In the consumer domain, we now feature custom items and last-minute products, and this is progress compared to the standardized consumption of the early twentieth century, when, for example, all cars were black. But just as in the very beginning of the assembly line, strains are already present, and people sometimes wonder if this is a better world. Making use of an employee's human capital does not necessarily mean that the world of production will be humanized. Increasing the choices of consumers solves some problems, but it raises new ones that may be harder to solve. The consumer who is offered every conceivable shade of blue is completely without recourse when the director of a good school refuses to enroll her child, or when she learns that someone close to her has fallen ill. It is actually in the nature of the goods that affect "human capital" (health, education, or territory) to be "public" in the sense that they must be produced by communities rather than by individuals. Witness David Landes's explanation of how in 1836 Nathan Rothschild died of common blood poisoning after attending his nephew's wedding.[3] The richest person in the world today still depends on medical advancements, which are essentially indivisible, despite any appearances to the contrary. This contributes to the challenge of contemporary human existence: hyperindividualism confronts radically public goods without achieving any kind of continuity. On the production side, workers no longer may have to obey a higher authority, but instead they may find themselves confronted with instructions from a computer program that banishes them to the new solitude of cyberspace. Alternatively, the recriminations of overly demanding clients spoiled by the "just in time" culture may remind a worker that "hell is other people."[4] The autonomy and the personal initiative required by the new productive world induce mental stress which replaces the physical fatigue of the worker's previous life of hard labor.

The key idea proposed by this book is that, just as prosperity is the primary reason for our leap from the previous modern age, paradoxically it is also prosperity that spotlights the resulting disillusionment in the present-day world. In paying workers seven times more today than yesterday, capitalism expects a worker to accomplish seven times more. Technology is there for just this result, but it is not a "neutral" assistant. In fact, contemporary humans are discovering that a society which is seven times richer more closely resembles an automobile capable of going seven times faster than it resembles someone 'strolling along with all the time in the world.

I   The New Wave

1 Modern Times: From Chaplin to Godard

When Aldous Huxley described a "brave new world" inspired by "his" modern times, he created a universe where nothing escaped the industrial machine. Serial production dictates its law to everything, including humans. Children and love stories are both produced on the assembly line. The new era has a new calendar in which the first year was 1909, the year the Model T was invented, and the heroes of the book curse the name of Ford when they are angry.[1]

Indeed, nothing better illustrates the expectations and the disillusions of the twentieth century than the phenomenon called Fordism, whose two essentials are standardized products (all cars are black) and mass production (to minimize unit costs). Although children never quite came to be produced on the assembly line, love stories did. What was to become the Hollywood motion picture industry took its cue from the automobile industry. Using this example, which is as good as any other, to look behind the scene for a moment, we will find an explanation for the tragic utopianism and naiveté that characterized the twentieth century.

The Stars

In order to join the world of serial production, a movie actor had to transform himself, becoming, as Edgar Morin said, a sort of mixed animal in which actors impose their personalities on their characters, who in turn impose their personalities on the actors.[2] The "star" thus created would be in demand, awaited at times with such fervor as Ava Gardner in *The Barefoot Contessa*, a character who first remains unseen and whom we see only through the perspective of others. The whole process of direction is actually constructed around the resolution of this contradiction: highlighting the renowned image of the star while conserving an essential portion of mystery. This allows actors to carry over the investment achieved through their earlier work as they proceed from film to film. Studios can thereby manufacture stars like new car models, and these investments are returned, thanks to iron-clad contracts, n as long a film career as possible.

The star constitutes the *design* of the product. Their mass production is subsequently accomplished through various genres of film. Gangster movies, westerns, costume epics, musicals, and comedies enable the consumers to identify ahead of time with the product they are going to consume. Thanks to this system, we generally "go to the movies" much more than we go to see a particular movie. The idea of the genre in film enables two imperatives to be reconciled: product standardization proceeding from manufacture and product differentiation proceeding from consumption. From the production perspective, genre divisions also permit the repeated use of the same sets and the same extras, and the hiring of specialized scriptwriters and directors.

Film writing must obey mass-production's imperatives. The head of EMI said that the goal of that company's filmmaking was to be comprehensible to a half-literate Uruguayan. The quest for a good story, for which numerous scriptwriters can be sacrificed, is the system's supreme virtue. He explained that writers, when lured by sums that are colossal in comparison to book or theater revenues, must fall into step, writing on demand and at fixed hours. Fitzgerald, Faulkner, Dos Passos, Chandler, West, Huxley, Parker, Cain, Saroyan, Bukowski, and others joined the system. Hollywood thus invented a new class of writer: salaried, unpublished, rewritten, and at times even erased or reduced to writing anonymously.[3]

Twentieth-Century Jobs

The flamboyant, tragic destinies of F. Scott Fitzgerald and Marilyn Monroe, who both drowned the sorrow of their newfound status as "artist" in alcohol and depression, show us the other side of paradise: the calamities of a system that wanted to "standardize" the world in order to make it better. In *Où va le travail humain?* (first published in

1950),[4] Georges Friedmann answered his own question by citing Antoine de Saint-Exupéry, author of *The Little Prince*, who asked, "Where are the United States going, and where are we ourselves going? . . . Man-robot, man-termite, man wavering between the assembly line and the pinochle table. Man expurgated of all his creative power and who no longer even knows, from the heart of his village, how to make up a dance or a song." In the twentieth century, making workers more efficient seemed to consist of doing the utmost to separate them as radically as possible from their humanity. "One principal advantage of (well-) conceived division of labor is that it makes a task less conscious while reducing the strain on nerve centers accordingly." These remarks from a corporate sociologist speak volumes about the idea of production's being organized by assembly-line practices. The entire history of the twentieth century could thus be retold as the dehumanization of the world. The obsession with using standardization to augment production volume ever further was the source of the twentieth century's pathologies in the most widely varied realms.

How could a century in which humans were largely free of the oppression of famine and in which they received education and universal health care have conceived of such a dehumanizing environment as the assembly line? The simplest way to answer this question is to acknowledge that there always exists a considerable disparity between productive and social spheres, i.e., between economy and society. Take the evolution of capitalism during the nineteenth century. One could say that the nineteenth century was a feudal world that was "exported" to the cities.[5] In the early days of factory work, schedules and customs remained the same as in the country: people got up early and went to bed late, and children worked. In part, the great misery of the life of a nineteenth-century worker was the transfer from the former peasant condition, easily illustrated by comparing statements about each of these two realities. The first of these is from Marx:

"That boy of mine," spoke one woman, "when he was 7 years old I used to carry him on my back to and through the snow, and he used to have 16 hours a day. . . . I have often knelt down to feed him as he stood by the machine, for he could not leave it or stop."[6]

The second, attributed to Vauban, describes rural life at the beginning of the eighteenth century:

To pull their plow, the peasants have to toil stooped almost to the ground like beasts. They have only small donkeys to pull it and some have been known to harness their scarcely clad wife alongside. They nourish themselves with rye bread without removing the bran which is heavy and as black as pitch. Indeed the children eat this bread as well; consequently a four-year-old girl has a belly as large as a pregnant woman's.[7]

Dante would find the tortures of his inferno far surpassed by these two descriptions: the poverty is the same; only the context has changed.

From a managerial point of view, the internal organization of the early factory system remained largely modeled on medieval production. Reminiscent of the world of the trade guild, groups of workers passed their expertise from

generation to generation. An excellent illustration of the
(first) industrial revolution is the iron and steel industry,
the workings of which Yves Lequin summarizes as follows:
"Empiricism still reigns with authority. It is a business of
the eye when the glassworker or the founder opens the
furnace because the smelt is ready to be extracted, the ear
carefully listening to the sounds of machines or of the steel
yard, the nose or the skin when one must distance oneself
from the furnace."[8] In fact the skilled worker remained the
heir to guilds' "secrets" until the end of the nineteenth century. Witness how in its early days, in a completely elitist
reading of its function, the principal American union, the
AFL (American Federation of Labor), restricted its mem-
bership to skilled worker, excluding unqualified laborers,
who most often were immigrants.[9]

With the advent of the assembly line, the landscape
changed radically. Taylor's book *The Principles of Scientific
Management* (1911) became the standard of the new industrial world. It brought the clock into the workshop, track-
ing the average time for each task and transforming the
worker into an automaton who ever after would be pow-
erless over his or her own job. Workers saw their contribu-
tions reduced to one identical movement, repeated
indefinitely; they were expropriated of their own "know-
how." Why did industry deprive itself of the wisdom of
the worker, accumulated in the course of centuries of
work? Simply because Taylor's system didn't want the
same workers as before. Fordism supported itself with the
illiterate masses and opened the door for the nineteenth-

century world to become a part of twentieth-century industrial capitalism. To simplify the comparison with what has been said of the early days of capitalism, we could say that the nineteenth-century society was exported to the factories of the twentieth century. Georges Friedmann notes in the American context that "the blacks, many of whom have recently come from the South, view as a promotion their massive entrance into large factories, their participation in imposing modern techniques in clean and well-paying jobs."[10] The assembly line was a pathway to integration that enabled blacks to escape the misery of the South. Benjamin Coriat recalls also that "the USA, more than any other country, had to pay for the absence of a sufficient number of skilled workers; and, even, until the 1960s, for the absence of workers, period." Between 1880 and 1915, no less than 15 million new immigrants were recorded in the United States. The balance between skilled and unskilled workers was completely shattered. Taylorism enabled unskilled laborers to enter the production world en masse.

The price to be paid for this "integration" would be high. One could say that Taylorism was characterized by excluding the worker from the very production process in which he or she was intended to be the main character. Workers were excluded in relation to the work: all the necessary conditions for the task are taken care of by the company. They were excluded in relation to knowledge: the worker was not there to think. They were excluded in relation to time: the schedules and the breaks were fixed.

They were excluded in relation to speaking: lateral communication was forbidden. And finally, summing up all the other exclusions, they were excluded from the sphere of cooperation: the worker was alone at his post, making his remuneration strictly private. Taylor was not unaware of the human dramas that his system would generate: he admitted seeing the anger in his worker friends' eyes. But he also thought that workers becoming richer thanks to this new productivity would enjoy the fruits of this new prosperity outside of work, that there would be a time for suffering and a time for pleasure. As Henri Weber said, parodying Daniel Bell's work *The Cultural Contradictions of Capitalism*, "one must be conscientious by day and a reveler by night."[11]

May 1968

But this schizophrenia had only one moment. The disparity between the economy and society made itself felt more and more. The time for "rectification" became inescapable. May 1968 can be interpreted as the time when the social bough supporting the modern industrial world finally broke. The baby boomers who instigated these uprisings refused to endure what they denounced as the hypocrisies of bourgeois society. "Never has a civilization reached such contempt for life, drowning in disgust; never has a generation exhibited such an enraged taste for living," the May '68 prophets wrote.[12] This passion for life was thrown up against the dehumanized world of the parents. In this regard, it is symptomatic that the book often referenced in premonitory literature of the day should be *Les Choses*, in which Georges Perec ridicules possession as the only way of life. Provoked (or perhaps sincerely), Michel Foucault concludes the great 1960s work *The Order of Things* with this line: "As the archaeology of our thought easily shows, man is an invention of recent date. And one perhaps nearing its end."[13] As Jean-Pierre LeGoff reiterated, the goal of May 1968 was to find out if men could still hope to find "a purpose that carries them, a word and actions in which they can be truly engaged."

The May 1968 protests were important for their universal impact upon the entire industrialized world. In the United States, in Western Europe, and in Japan, the movement at work was one and the same. And the red line that divided the revolution was simply a matter of generations. Youth rejected the world of their parents, which for that matter explained why the countries where this period was the most tumultuous were also those where the most serious matters in dispute were those concerning parents: Germany, Italy, and Japan.[11]

Curiously, the "humanistic" values behind May 1968 have not always been apparent to the people involved. This misunderstanding was most tragic for all those who came to establish themselves as workers in factories. They discovered that the workers resented their young bourgeois freedom. For the workers themselves, the uprisings were a question of rejecting factory work and the general situation of the worker. The best proof of this is a film from June 1968 showing the desperation of the young woman at the Wonder factory who refused to go back to work.[15] We can even say that our "modern times" are born of these tears.

The cinema, which showed what assembly-line tactics could do for industry, had the best view of these implications. At the beginning of the 1960s, Hollywood was already experiencing the preliminary blows of May 1968. The style it had invented was exhausted. The public no longer accepted films lacking, as François Truffaut would later say, even the least bit of truth, where "the actors' clothes, for example, are never wrinkled, their hair never undone."[16] The cinematic "new wave," modeled in the image of the French May 1968 uprisings, perfectly embodied the new questioning of the Hollywood-style film. "For my part," Truffaut wrote, "after having seen three thousand films in ten years, I can no longer stand the false, insipidly pretty love scenes of Hollywood cinema, as well as those rude, licentious, and no less contrived examples in French films." And Jean-Luc Godard chimed in: "We cannot pardon you for never filming girls as we know and love them, boys as we see them every day, parents as we scorn or admire them, children as they astonish us or as they only spark indifference, in short, things as they really are."[17]

This "refusal of convention, this burden of parody that distanced spectators to the point where they could no longer find their naive adherence to the codes of genre"[18] would hit Hollywood head-on, but the industry would not really die from these criticisms. Its economic strength would remain intact, and it would make the utmost use of that strength in epic productions, where its principal advantages continue to lie. However, Jacqueline Nacache concludes, not without some nostalgia, that "today the Hollywood-style cinema is like an orphan who would have inherited a huge fortune only to squander it in the hope of finding its parents."

Computers and Freedom

The evolution experienced by the industrial world since the beginning of the 1970s is difficult to understand without seeing that its pioneers are those same baby boomers who led the charge in 1968. Manuel Castells summarizes this evolution: "Universities were the principal agents of diffusion and social innovation. The young people who frequent them discover and adopt new ways of thinking, of direction, of acting, and of communicating."[19] By various detours, it was through computer science that students raised in the anti-establishment culture of the 1960s American campus would find a way to shatter the world of standardization created by their parents. Taking the same metaphor we used in relation to the preceding revolutions, we can say that baby boomers coming from the universities would be exported to the new world of production via the computer revolution.

The computer saga[20] unfolded between 1960 and the 1980, but the fact that such a short period of time could

generate such an upheaval is anything but astonishi
Joseph Schumpeter explained that innovations ordina
come in clusters. The first industrial revolution, associa
with the steam engine, took shape in scarcely a dec
(the 1770s); the second, associated with electricity, g
birth to a plethora of innovations between 1880 and 1
"Our" industrial revolution, that associated with comp
ers, "began" in 1971, when Intel invented the micropro
sor, whose power, according to "Moore's Law," wc
double every 18 months. In 1976, Steve Wozniak
Steve Jobs launched the first personal computer, the A
II. IBM countered in 1981 with the commercializatio
its own version of the micro-computer. In 1984 A
counterattacked with the Macintosh, which opened
era of the user-friendly computer. This competitior
which a third opportunist, Microsoft, would be the
ner) allowed computers to become accessible to every
and to break out of the cumbersome guardianship o
computer "professionals" who had reigned suprem
the 1970s.

It is possible to measure the "sociology" of these dis
eries by following the events that give birth to
Internet. In 1969 the US Defense Advanced Rese
Projects Agency (DARPA) set up a revolutionary con
nication network whose aim was to protect American
itary communications from disruption by nuclear str
This system was used more and more by academics
were under contract to the Pentagon. It entered int
public domain thanks to the invention of the mode

2 Burnout

The information age is a radical counterpoint to mass consumption such as it was conceived earlier in the twentieth century. The obsession with standardizing everything, the mark of the past century, has now been replaced with the equally obsessive plan to de-standardize work as well as products. We expect workers to be versatile and multiskilled; we expect production runs to be short; we expect products to be fabricated "just in time" and practically custom-made. To stay with audio-visual examples, one can say that "channel surfing" has become the new motto for our contemporary modern world, and that the next Aldous Huxley will likely make the remote control the symbol of a world whose inhabitants will curse it when they are upset.

Scarce are the television viewers who have decided what they are going to watch before sitting down in front of the screen. Most now click the remote control until they find something they like, and often even then will continue to change channels all evening. Similarly, workers must click from one task to another. The executive who types his own letters or answers his own electronic mail, the switchboard operator who makes photocopies, the hotel desk clerk who also prepares for guests to check out the next morning, the typist for a small business who is also in charge of the supply order, the mechanic who sells insurance policies or offers to buy your car, the bank officer who opens an account and offers (based on information gathered from you) various financial products: so many examples showcase the new variety of tasks.[1] The specialization of the Fordist world is being supplanted by polyvalence.

Paradoxes of Clicking

To grasp this new nature of work, let us first return to what Adam Smith said of the division of work in general. For the author of *The Wealth of Nations*, the main source of worker productivity is the specialization of tasks. The more one insists that a worker be confined strictly to one given sort of work, the more one can be sure that the worker will do it efficiently.[2] Revisiting this idea in their article "Specialization and Coordination," Gary Becker and Kevin Murphy expose the dilemma of human activities as follows: If we accept Smith's views of the benefits of the division of labor, how can we understand the reasons for his limits?[3] Taking an example from the university, imagine a researcher who limited his or her knowledge to a very thin slice of material—for example, the history of

France in the first half of 1789. The researcher's competence in this narrow field would certainly be precise, but various inconveniences would result from the extreme specialization: in order to apply fully the knowledge collected on the first half of 1789, one must be able to *coordinate* it with the knowledge of others who specialize in the 6 months preceding and following that period and, by degrees, with the history of the whole eighteenth century. The material and intellectual limits to this coordination process explain why each specialist in a certain domain must be a generalist in another domain, whether to better communicate his or her knowledge or to better use the knowledge of others.

For now, let us interpret the computer revolution as a manner of reducing communication costs. Say that computers are to the circulation of ideas what electricity is to the transmission of energy. If we follow the explanation of Becker and Murphy, computers should entail a *rise* in specialization, just as electricity led to an increase the division of work. Each person should actually further specialize his or her field of knowledge, following the argument that, thanks to specialization, it becomes easier to call on the knowledge of others. How can we understand the economic paradox of "clicking"—i.e., that there is an apparent contradiction between the reduction of coordination costs and the decrease in the specialization of work? How can one explain that numerous tasks, previously disjointed and specialized, hereafter are to done by the same person? Answers can be given at several levels.[4]

First, we can say that the coordination of tasks has itself become a new productive task which, by its very nature, cannot be specialized (as in mathematics it has been shown that the set of all sets is not a set). "Browsing" the World Wide Web in search of information (the ultimate form of which is never known in advance) the way a television viewer clicks around searching for a good program is a necessarily "polyvalent" activity that is difficult if not impossible to delegate.

Second, we can interpret the new polyvalence of the computer world on another axis. Consider the example of the executive who types his or her own documents, thereby absorbing a portion of the tasks that in the past fell to a secretary. It can be said that here computers participate in the rationing of clerical work, by expropriating from secretaries a portion of their knowledge. Here, the computer *destroys* old jobs by putting the corresponding knowledge into the public domain. The polyvalence of work is possible only because one of the tasks (the role of the secretary) has been made commonplace or has disappeared.

A third explanation of computer-oriented polyvalence deals with the fact that the new world of production is accompanied by leaner hierarchical structures. Employees are no longer under the control of their bosses; they are regulated by computer programs.[5] There is no longer a white-collar manager who gives orders to a blue-collar worker; there is, however, someone with a collar of an intermediary color, and that person is consumed by a problem that he or she must resolve. The reduction of communication costs here results in the destruction of tasks connected to old ways of transmitting orders. As with our image of the secretary, it is simpler to say that certain executive tasks have been liquidated by the computer revolution.

Another essential principle that explains the new polyvalence of work is the hunting down of stoppages. The hotel night clerk who prepares guests' bills for the next morning patently takes up two tasks with no informational ties and without hierarchical relations. The fact that he is asked to execute both tasks is proof of a new obsession with the organization of work: to hunt down wastefulness, to no longer pay people for doing nothing. As Philippe Askenazy illustrated,[6] the systematic rise in work-related accidents that accompany industrial reorganizations is the proof that a new "Stakhanovism" is at work in today's production world. Against the old model's obsession with always having more task specialization, the new regime will seek to raise productivity by pushing as many tasks as possible on one person.

To explain this intensification of work, we can say, first of all, that computers make it easier to click from one task to another. (For example, the night clerk clicks his mouse to immediately access the accounting software.) It is easier to do two things at once than it used to be. More precisely, one can say that computers transform the professional knowledge of each person into assets of the company, whereas in the past it would have remained the knowledge of the individual worker. Thus the standardization begun by Fordism is pursued further via computers and the characteristics of their use.[7] But there is far more than this technological fact. Everything that contributes to making one person absorb the task of another saves on costs, which have more impact today than they did in the past simply because workers are better paid today.

The proof of this principle is found in a simple statement: The higher one rises on the revenue scale, the more one may be overloaded with work. Without necessarily inspiring tears, studies on the subject show that often managers would like to work and earn less. There are also a higher number of managers than other employees who feel that they are underpaid for the work that they do! As has been noted in *The Economist*, not without humor: "Their natural advantages (luxurious dining room . . .) have disappeared for the most part. In their everyday life, they travel much less, they eat however they can in airplanes. . . ." Indeed, according to this study, managers take on responsibility that in the past was shared by three to five people. In effect, they themselves are subject to the narrowing of hierarchical structures, and the physical and (especially) mental price they pay often results in a shortened career. Their fortunes made, they stop working earlier and earlier (often to become consultants).

What makes this intensification of work particularly difficult stems from the fact that it does not keep each of the various tasks thereafter done by the same person from remaining quite specialized. An executive who types her own letters is no less specialized than her predecessor; she simply adds her work as a secretary to her work as an executive. We could thus say that the computer revolution imitates the reversal of the fallow at the dawn of the eighteenth century, when the peasants learned to rotate crops to avoid having to leave fields uncultivated every 3 years. Today it is the reversal of the human fallow that is sought. This is what caused *The Economist* to say that business had become a "toxic world."

Lessons in Fordism

We must return to the causes of the crisis in the Fordist organizational model, a model that constructed a productive world based on the idea that a workers could lose themselves in their assigned tasks, to measure the whole scope of the shift that is being produced in the organization of labor. Even from a strictly economic standpoint, the programmed boredom of someone in front of a machine carries a sizable cost: the worker who becomes bored suffers, becoming distracted in the face of the tasks he or she is asked to accomplish. Absenteeism and turnover quickly become the wounds resulting from "the scientific organization of work." The very concept of assembly-line work means that it is vulnerable to the defection of any one of its parts, and assembly-line failure rates are indeed spectacular. Quiet sabotage or simply distracted workers exact a considerable price. Witness the high percentage of those whose task is supervising the work of others. A US

Department of Health study found that 40 percent of production losses were due to absenteeism, sabotage, and work conflicts.

From the very beginning of Fordism, this problem was clear to company directors. First they turned to psychologists, who explained that an "affective" environment must be created, especially in forming the executive team. Attempts were made to reaffirm that the human unit must be respected, that the worker is not simply another machine. Workers' family problems were taken into account (counseling).[8] To ward off the suffering of the lone worker before his machine, Henry Ford realized he must do much more. What? Double their salary. In 1914, Ford offered to increase his employees' pay to $5 a day. The day after the offer, more than 10,000 workers squeezed against the gates of the Ford factories looking for jobs. Analysts concluded that "this was a good deal for Ford." Workers' attachment to the company, their motivation, and their productivity all increased. According to the calculations of Ford's human resources manager, John Lee, worker productivity went up 51 percent in 1914. Absenteeism was reduced by half, and workers were considerably more "docile."[9]

According to Ford himself, this salary increase was the most tremendous cost-reduction measure he ever enacted. His respite, however, would be of short duration. He quickly realized that in fact it was not enough to double salaries in order to increase workers' productivity. What really counted was that workers be paid double what they would be paid *elsewhere*. So the rest of the economy, from Hollywood to McDonald's, aligned itself on Fordist standards, and Ford's long-run failure is unavoidable: the effect of the salary increases on productivity was condemned to run out of steam. Contrary to what the prophets thought, this process could not create a better world. It could only be one chapter in the history of capitalism.

The *e* Factor

The crisis of Fordism revealed that worker productivity is not an intangible fact set by education or experience. It depends upon *cooperation*, whether desired or sustained, between the workers and the company. A worker's "latent" productivity will never be clearly revealed without his or her assent. There is always a disparity between the work paid for and the work actually accomplished, which depends on the *effort* deployed by the employee to accomplish his or her task. Work science (ergonomics) has devised a term: the opposition between the "prescribed" work (the task asked of the worker) and the "real" work (what is actually accomplished). The "real" work depends, to speak as Lacanians, on what the specialists designate as *e*: the workers' secret effort at the task, a measure of their assent.[10]

To grasp this notion, in the course of the 1980s, economists developed the *efficiency wage* theory, which has since become one axis of labor market thought.[11]

Originally, this theory was founded on an observation made for developing economies in the 1950s: By increasing workers' wages in poor countries, one succeeded in increasing their productivity more than proportionally. It is therefore profitable to pay workers "well," for the simple reason that, in doing so, they are permitted to be well fed, well housed, and well cared for, which, all in all, is good for their productivity. Transposed to industrial countries, this theory corresponds to Ford's realization that paying employees better makes money for their bosses.[12] Effectively, in exposing workers to the risk of losing a "good" wage (that is, a wage they could not expect to find elsewhere), they are prompted to cooperate: to play the (constrained) game of mobilizing their effort. Nonetheless, the wedge that must therefore be created between a "productive" worker's wage and that of the "rest" of society immediately makes apparent the necessity of an opposition between a "modern" sector (where wages are high) and an "archaic" sector (where they are weak and snatched away from the workers by the world's modernization). The efficiency wage theory thus unveils the necessary limit to the extension of the first sector in relation to the second. As we effectively saw, Fordism necessarily deregulates itself from the moment it penetrates the ensemble of the layers of society. As a result, the duality between the modern and archaic worlds then bears rethinking.

We can clarify the scope of this theory by looking again at Marxism. The economic theory of Marx is constructed on a fundamental idea: the distinction between work and what Marx calls "the labor power." For Marx, the worker is paid what it costs the worker to live, to "reproduce" his "labor power." For this price, nonetheless, the worker can work more. For example, if the equivalent of 4 hours' work is necessary to feed the worker, he or she can work very hard for 10 hours; this allows the boss to pocket a surplus, which measures the difference between the two. This crucial distinction between work and the force of work is in a sense conserved by modern theories, but with a bit of wordplay we can say that it is reversed today. For today's theories, one really can buy only the "work"—that is, the number of hours during which it is expected that a worker will be bound to a task. Yet what is expected of individual workers is the yielding of their "force of work"—that is, that secret effort, the e of economic theories, which will make their work efficient.

Following this distinction, it can be said that the computer revolution makes for a more radical monitoring structure than was present under Fordism. The workers' autonomy—their *empowerment*, which consists of imparting upon them larger responsibility—is in fact the way to make them directly accountable for their role in the company. In the language of ergonomics, the contemporary modern world has radically changed the nature of that which is "prescribed." It is no longer physical effort or the attention brought to a task that is at issue; rather, it is the worker's very subjectivity.

The New Worker Condition

That the motion picture industry applied the principles of the assembly line to their industry should alert us against the naive idea that technology is the sole instigator in the evolution of labor organization. Nothing, speaking strictly technologically, obligated film producers to be inspired by the assembly line. It was not technology that Hollywood imported from the Ford plants; it was a certain way of organizing human work. In the same way, the new way of organizing work in the computer revolution corresponds to something quite different than a technical necessity. The ideas of hunting down work stoppages, of polyvalence, and of flat hierarchies were tested well before the appearance of portable computers. These ideas were born in Toyota plants in Japan during the 1960s.

The great transformation introduced by what has since been called "Toyotaism" was offering workers much more flexibility in performing tasks. In this system, a worker reporting a defect of some sort can appeal to his or her immediate colleagues instead of to the superiors, thereby correcting breakdowns more quickly. Workers also are asked to "re-program" the production line themselves to change paint colors according to need. In the Toyota system, information is passed on by means of posters placed in the same boxes where the workers indicate the pieces needed to fill clients' orders in real time. This is far from the exchange of information permitted today by computer technology, but the principle is already there: the "lowest" level in the production channels sends information to the upper levels and becomes an active player in the production process. The Japanese-American economist Masahiko Aoki summarizes the contribution of the Japanese company as follows: "Whereas American industrialization has generated an exceptionally high degree of job differentiation and attached a high value to specialization, the Japanese work organization seems to rely more on the versatility of workers and flexibility in job demarcation."[13]

Many Americans had long thought that the United States would not catch up to Japan in "quality," so untrusting were they of American workers. It took the arrival of "transplants" (Japanese subsidiaries) in the United States to convince them that it would be possible for American firms to operate the same way. "Quality circles" that enabled each worker to remedy problems as they arose with the support of his or her co-workers allowed at once for "enrichment" of the work experience and for considerable improvement of the "final quality" of the product. The "rate of failure" was reduced by two-thirds in the Toyota plants.

For all that, the line worker has not disappeared. In 1991 nearly 600,000 workers were still on French assembly lines. But the factory working class is being progressively destroyed by the automation of production. In the period 1982–1997, a million laborer positions were eliminated in France. According to data presented by Dominique Goux and Eric Maurin, the French chemical industry got rid of half its unskilled positions.[14] In 1982 there were still more than 100,000 unskilled workers in French metallurgy, 170,000 in the garment industry, and nearly 100,000 in textiles. Today these three categories together represent no more than 30,000 jobs. However, as Goux and Maurin say, "the decline of the working class is not only quantitative; it is above all qualitative. Unskilled workers are no longer found in teams, on vast 1960s production lines. They are scattered in the cleaning and surveillance industries, to whom the new industrial establishments entrust their premises each night, after closing." In the 1960s, three-fourths of French blue-collar jobs were in manufacturing. Today, more than half of such jobs are in the service industry, and in much smaller companies than before. The new positions for blue-collars are as repairers, operators, and maintenance workers. For many of them, client contact has become frequent; nearly 40 percent of laborers declare that their work is directly dependent on client or public demands. The new working class, more often recruited in giant supermarkets than in the automobile industry, suffers everywhere the pressure of the "client."

Live Work

Toyotaism's objective was to obtain the assent of the worker, thereby implicating the worker in the organization of work. The psychological effect of this objective is perfectly summarized by the report of France's Agence Nationale de Conditions du Travail: "Management practices like quality circles and expression groups present the company as a place of action opening its petals to the wage-earner. Yet the observed forms of polyvalence, which reward excellence and individual performance, and increase rotation between the most demanding work-stations, have devastating effects, especially frustration, isolation, and competition."[15] In the future, mental health crises would be a major cause of absenteeism.

In effect, everything proceeds as if our contemporary modern world had generated a tremendous reversal of the burden of proof. Now it is no longer the responsibility of the company to watch over its workers; it is the work-ers' responsibility to demonstrate to the company that they have really done their work. In the words of Jean Baudrillard, "Today individuals are less alienated by the fact that everything is known about them than by the fact that they are requested to know everything about them-selves. This is the principle of a new and definitive servi-tude." There is truly a major break with the previous industrial organization. Companies want to pay for "real" work, not for hours spent at work. It is as if the com-pany's protective function in relation to market competi-tion rules had been rendered volatile. Competition is internal at the company, or externalized to subcontrac-tors, but it exists everywhere. Stress becomes the way to regulate post-Fordist society. Living work becomes live work and the limit to the new labor organization of work is burnout.

This trend is exhibited in the recent history of mental illnesses. As Alain Ehrenberg illustrates, "standard" neuroses connected to conflicts with various figures of authority (fathers, bosses, . . .) no longer make up the majority of mental illnesses.[16] They have given way to depression that stems from fears of not being good enough, of being unable to "perform" what is demanded of one. As Danièle and Robert Linhart tell us, there is no doubt that the new ideas of "autonomy, initiative, and cooperation have as their counterparts suffering, confusion, uneasiness, powerlessness, stress, and fear."[17] In today's world, it is no longer machines that break down; it is men and women.

3 The New Consumer Society

"Civilization is a limitless multiplication of unnecessary necessities," as Mark Twain said.[1] Does the critique of the "consumer society" signal the reaching of another limit? One reading of the "paradox of clicking" idea can be perfectly tailored to fit this example: Television viewers try in vain to escape the monotonous schedule of programs which no longer give them the feelings they got from the first TV shows they saw. In this interpretation, new forms of consumption can only be the swan song of a society that will soon cease to work for lack of the subterfuges that permitted it to grow in the first place.

However, it is not clear that the "consumer society" critique really specifies the saturation of human "needs." As Robert Rochefort tells us, "consumption is quite often denounced by those who cannot bear the vulgarity of the democratization ideal, which is brought by the consumer society, though quite imperfectly."[2] Nonetheless, a more generous utopia is hidden behind the idea of an "end of consumption." Engels thought that socialism was within

reach; that workers would house themselves, clothe themselves, and have plenty to eat; that soon each person
would be able to consume "according to his needs."
Alfred Sauvy tells of an astonishing experience touching
this subject: People asked "How large an increase of your
income would permit you to satisfy your needs?"
answered, on average, that it would take an increase of
approximately one-third. When asked again 10 years later,
when their income had in fact grown by one-third, the
same people answered, again, "one-third more."[3]

A typical way to approach consumption is to consider it
motivated by the desire to do better than or at least as well
as one's neighbors—to do "like the Joneses," in the words
of the consumption theorist James Duesenberry. As much
as the satisfaction of this desire is "possible" (that is, as
much as individual destinies remain tied by a common
dynamic), the consumer society appeases the frustrations it
creates. But what will happen if the inequalities widen?
What can the individual do if the Joneses get ahead of him
or her? Robert Castel explains that the "wage-earning society" functions well only if each group anticipates catching
up with the others.[4] Can we say that by the measure of this
last criterion that the consumer society is in crisis?

It is indisputable that the question of consumption
arises in terms other than those that were apropos in the
1950s and the 1960s. Indeed, in those days it was custom-
ary to measure the distance between two social classes by
the "delay" of one relative to the other with respect to the
consumption of any particular good.[5] For example, at the

beginning of the 1950s, only 1 percent of the population was in possession of a television set; 20 years later, laborers have as many audio-visual devices as executives do. Furthermore, the proportion of senior executives in 1959 who had cars is the same as the number of agricultural households that possessed them in 1970. From such comparisons, we have become used to counting in years the distance separating farmers or laborers from executives for each type of good. We can therefore say what the delay is for the most disadvantaged categories: 15 years for cars, 9 years for refrigerators, 7 years for washing machines, and so on.

But we would be at great pains today to calculate the distance of social classes by such a "delay index." The vast majority of contemporary Western households are "equipped" with all the goods that the late twentieth century and the early twenty-first century can provide. Now the margins make themselves apparent within each product category by the evident quality. The inequalities, no longer temporary, are seemingly becoming more and more permanent. All individuals can attest to the gap that separates them from those who are better off, without believing that they might someday catch up.

Before extending this question further, we can argue that the idea according to which wealth is simply a desire to be richer than our neighbors offers a very limited view of human history. Why is it said that welfare recipients are poor? It is not because they suffer from not being as rich as others; it is because they are poor with respect to things we consider essential in this day and age: health, the secure intimacy of a clean residence, education for one's children, and so on. It is not a matter of "superfluous" needs. For example, having enough to eat is obviously a precursor to being well cared for, but this does not mean that eating is necessary while taking care of oneself is superfluous. What a paradox it is to speak of the saturation of consumption at a time when so many people are up against the difficulty of accessing a decent life!

For that matter, how high should we go on the income ladder to find a household whose necessities could be said to be saturated with the necessities? Thinking in these terms, we can, without too much trouble, predict that the consumer society still has good days ahead, so far do laborers, employees, intermediate professions or executives seem from the idea that all their needs have been met. In this regard, let us keep in mind certain figures. The "average" French salary is $20,000 a year, meaning that this is what the salary would be if all French people earned exactly the same amount. The salary of workers and employees (nearly identical these days) is $15,500 per year for the former and $16,000 for the latter, which represents 60 percent of the population. Executives earn $35,000 on average and intermediate professions earn $22,000; these two categories represent 30 percent of the population (10 percent and 20 percent, respectively). If we could wave a magic wand or stage a cultural revolution and render all salaries identical, then the laborers' situation would improve by 20 percent.

Schumpeter said after World War II that if capitalism managed to prolong its previous growth patterns (and indeed it did much better) then all the socialist utopias would be realized by 1970. But here we are in 2003, and Schumpeter's dreams have yet to come to fruition. Like Engels before him, Schumpeter fell victim to the illusion of the worker who thinks that one day he will attain the elusive one-third of wealth that he needs to be happy.

But the initial question still awaits a response: How can it be that the spectacular prosperity of today's societies never succeeds in absorbing our desire to consume? Indeed, why does it seem to make consumption as unsatisfying as ever? How can we understand this amazing ability of the capitalist civilization to enlarge the sphere of its needs indefinitely?

The simplest way to approach this mystery is by understanding first of all how consumption evolves, going from the poorest to the richest person. Doubling the average consumer's income, after all, means only that an income of $20,000 per year is increased to $40,000; there is nothing here that defies the imagination. Family budgets allow for differences in consumption from household to household to be represented quite distinctly depending on their various incomes.[6] It is certainly no mystery that the laborer would answer the question "What would you do with your money if your income doubled?" as follows: "I would buy a car twice as expensive and a house twice as expensive, and in the house I would put furnishings twice as expensive. I would increase my spending on groceries by only 40 percent, freeing up some resources that would let me increase my leisure spending by about 50 percent." In short, aside from leisure, today laborers with more funds at their disposal generally do not acquire new goods, as they did in the middle of the twentieth century. Rather, they augment the quality of goods they already possess—for example, they exchange a small car for a big one and a vacation in the countryside for one at a Mediterranean resort.

Sometimes such comparisons are tricky in that they indicate the effects of increased income on an individual (a laborer whose income matches that of an executive). They do not indicate how a society's consumption would evolve were the income of *each* of its members to be doubled.[7] In effect there exists a crucial difference between the evolution of a household that becomes richer than its neighbors and the evolution of an entire society. Only certain "elementary" goods (such as food and, perhaps more surprising, leisure) follow a parallel route in regard to the individual and the collective trends of behavior.

Conversely, if we examine clothing, we find radically opposite evolutions. As it becomes richer, a nation like France devotes less and less of its income to clothing. Contrarily, an individual becoming richer devotes an increasingly large part of his or her income to clothing. Individual differential enrichment provides the means to dress well, to mark one's place in society by visible exterior signs. This "ostentatious consumption" also manifests itself, to a lesser extent, in expenditures for automobiles, household furnishings, and appliances.

Health is the exact opposite of luxury goods. In effect, society as a whole must become richer in order for each individual's consumption of medical care to increase. In contrast to clothing, which could be considered consumption for snobs, health is a good that is only desired in social terms, for the simple reason that, for the most part, it can only be produced socially on an equal scale. But health is not the only good that functions this way. Housing (to a lesser extent) and environmental quality can only be consumed publicly, for the most part, and can be referred to as "social goods."

We can see taking shape here something that allows us to understand the evolution of consumption, a skewing of subsistence spending toward leisure expenses, which correspond to elementary necessities where private and social evolutions coincide. Conspicuous consumer goods (traditional ones such as clothing or modern one such as cars) are items of social fascination that feed—indefinitely—the frustration of the individual. In the final analysis, consumption of "social" goods (health, environment, housing, education) can only progress in unison, and it needs a common social framework in order to prosper. In sum, we can say that the consumer is one-third the "naive" consumer who wants to satisfy "elementary needs," one-third the "cynical" consumer who wants to outdo the neighbors, and one-third the "civic" consumer who can only imagine consumption collectively. Our consumers are always all three of these modes at the same time.

The Future of Consumption

It is becoming possible to understand the "crisis" of the consumer society, and the intimate connection it has to the crisis of mass production. Cars, plumbing, and washing machines, all goods associated with twentieth-century mass consumption, are at the same time elementary necessities, ostentatious goods (for keeping up with the Joneses), and social necessities. As Rochefort said, these are actually "semi-collective" goods which are consumed above all at home with family.[8] In the early 1950s, a television set in the middle of a living room was a typical example. In those days, a TV set effectively marked the social territory of household that possessed it; by the 1970s, every household had one. But television is also a social good, insofar as it presents the same program to entire families, who then serve as an effective relay between the public and private sectors. It is this union of opposites that is broken into pieces today.

The progressive saturation of domestic furnishing rates opens the consumer good to a new, more individualistic logic. This new logic casts off the semi-collective logic founded on the act of household equipment that was at the heart of the previous period. Thus, Rochefort writes, "objects are becoming mobile, coming out of the residence, accompanying the individual in his movement. It is no longer a question of accepting the division of roles implied by the semi-collective logic of past decades." The evolution of production modes accompanies, even encourages, this evolution. "Automation and flexibility, which replaced Taylorism and standardization, permit small-scale production to the point of arriving at a near-personalization of things. The same way that Fordism was the meeting between the production mode and the largely uniform mass consumption mode, Toyotaism was an *organization of production adapted to a prodigious change in the mode of consumption*." Such is indeed one of the essential effects of Toyotaism: acting on the fact that standardized mass production had reached its limits, and that the time for "flexible" consumption had arrived.

The change of consumption to a more individualistic logic is only one aspect of the problem. Currently, the great products of modern consumption (health care and the education of children) are effectively social products. They can only be consumed collectively, and usually under the aegis of public agents. All these items of consumption are the hidden mark of the twentieth century. In breaking out of the object world, people discover in themselves a new humanity, which absorbs a growing portion of their productive time. It is the tension between these two aspects that poses today's problem. Never before has the opposition between the public and private spheres of consumption been so pronounced. Never before has the consumer, accustomed to the idea that one dictates one's own choices to producers, been so incapacitated as when he must choose a school for his children or as when she must acquiesce to a doctor who proposes that she have surgery.

Pushing this parallel to the limit, we can affirm that this dissociation between the private and public sides of consumption mimics the evolution of the family. As Irène Théry has shown, the family fuses together two different functions: love stories and lines of parentage.[9] The family is only in "crisis" in relation to the first of these: no one wants to prolong failed love stories "in the name of the family" any more. But the parental function remains absolutely intact, even is paradoxically reinforced, owing to the fact of this dissociation. Concern for children is stronger than ever.

This dissociation makes way for contradictory attitudes. At times, the consumer, aspiring to align the production of social goods with the production of other goods, reacts by re-implicating the production of public goods. Yet this "option" is immediately accompanied by greater fears as soon as one tries to reform (or to save money on) health care or education. Contemporary humans are divided between these two opposing components of consumption—between the new consumer society (which offers "custom-made" goods) and public consumption (which offers essentially the same goods, such as health care and education, to all). It is hard to live in a society that exalts differences at the same time that a good half of the decisions to be made are by nature public choices.

4 From Financial Capital to Human Capital

The new world of production is taken as a synonym for neo-liberalism, and cyber-world pioneers are frequently denounced for their collusion with it. The ideology of Margaret Thatcher and Ronald Reagan is put in the same sack as the libertarian utopia of information-age pioneers, the sources of which are at once anterior and quite distinct ideologically. Is it an inescapable necessity for the computer revolution to swing back and forth between traders and hackers?

It should not surprise us that the information revolution finds its "spontaneous" ideology in neo-liberalism. The revolution values the part over the whole; it lauds autonomy over hierarchy; it transfers the weight of social construction to individuals who are more and more dissociated from society. In this regard, our current industrial revolution happens to be in a situation exactly opposite the preceding one. In its time Fordism had just as spontaneously emerged onto a totalitarian ideology. It is said that Ford himself was fascinated by Hitler, and it is well known that Hitler admired Ford's work. For that matter, the only economic program of Nazism was to build cars and roads (at least until the re-armament program of 1936).[1]

Fordism nevertheless succeeded in turning aside from its totalitarian leanings. Under truly tragic conditions, it abruptly turned on itself, serving as the foundation of the postwar social-democratic balance. Will the same occur with the computer revolution? Will this movement also be turned away from its neo-liberal course? If so, on which axes, and at the cost of what transformations? This is a vast question, and we will attack it progressively.

The Era of Financial Capital

There are several ways to illustrate the relationship between the new paradigm of production and neo-liberalism, such as deregulation and the decrease in unions, etc. But doubtless the simplest way to begin is with the new role of financial markets in the organization of production. The 1980s and the 1990s witnessed a brutal intrusion in the management of companies by financial markets, a phenomenon for which previous management methods had not prepared us.

Financial markets first played a fairly spectacular role in financing the computer revolution itself. A number of successes among the "start-ups" of the cyber world are to their credit. Without the NASDAQ, many new companies—including Microsoft—would never have existed.

This financial market "face of light" shows us little of the other aspect of the financial revolution: the new management of companies. Within just a few years, the game rules of capitalism were suddenly transformed, and the financial profitability became the golden rule of contemporary capitalism. The break with the old rules, progressively developed over the course of the twentieth century, is dramatic.

Throughout the century, "managerial" capitalism asserted itself. "Managers," directors who also were simply wage earners of the company, took over direction of business in the name of an industrial imperative where shareholder satisfaction was never the primary concern. Indeed, the only objective of the "managers" was to help companies become as large as possible in order to attain "scale economies," like a movie star who acts in several films, amortizing the sale of new products over the largest number possible.

The margin dug between this type of organization and our contemporary modern world will never be better appraised than in Galbraith's book *The New Industrial State*, every page of which seems to describe *a contrario* the world we are entering today. Galbraith describes twentieth-century managerial capitalism in words that merit repeating in full:

The men who now head the great corporations are unknown. Not for a generation have people outside Detroit and the automobile industry known the name of the current head of General Motors. In the manner of all men, he must produce identification when paying by check. So with Ford, Standard Oil, and General Dynamics. The men who now run the large corporations own no appreciable share of the enterprise. They are selected not by the stockholders but, in the common case, by a Board of Directors which narcissistically they selected themselves.[2]

In this time of great stock market battles, when share-holder values have asserted themselves and have created a new landscape for modern capitalism, it is astonishing to hear the echo of industrial capitalism from less than 30 years ago. What storm was then brewing on the earth? The certainty with which Galbraith presents the stability of the old system amuses and astonishes us. Would it have been able to continue functioning so well indefinitely?

In his postwar book *Capitalism, Socialism, and Democracy*, Schumpeter asks whether capitalism can survive and answers with a surprising "No."[3] Contrary to Galbraith's thoughts quoted above, this response was guided by the idea that capitalism would not survive the bureaucratiza-tion process generated by managerial capitalism. Schumpeter explained that capitalism needed entrepre-neurs who would take risks and who would destroy acquired income. With the bureaucratization of capitalism, the "entrepreneurs" (not to be confused with "managers") were condemned to disappear, and along with them inno-vation and economic growth.

Schumpeter's diagnosis illustrates what has come of cap-italism in recent years. It has survived well; however, it has done so by crushing managerial capitalism, which has been replaced by a new "patrimonial capitalism" that marks the revenge of the shareholders on the wage earners.[4]

The Nature of a Firm

The simplest way to approac[h]
capitalism and the transforma[tion]
briefly to the economic theory o[f]
various pioneers (Coase, Will[iamson]
writings on the "nature of the fi[rm]
sively richer.[5] "What is a firm?" [is]
tion. A firm is where producti[on]
constituted of capital, workers, [and]
it is all that and significantly m[ore]
called social relations and what [is]
contracts"—that is, a series of u[n]
means to work, to obey, and to [
From the employer's side, there a[re]
what it means to "be just" co[
obligations, career profiles, etc.

This "knot of implicit contracts[
constructed in time and in histor[y
D'Iribarne and his collaborators t[
erences to what is "just" and wh[at
countries. For example, when a [
Swedish colleague to advance hi[
himself justified as long as he m[
his colleague will think him simp[
tion is reversed when a French p[
American; it is the former who w[
gant when the latter thinks he is n[
matically."[7] This example and tho[

that w[
ductio[n

Foll[ow
to int[e
which
and L[
to cre[
the in[
For e[
career
rising
more
loyalt[
from
salari[
whos[
perso[
funct[
tial t[
appa[
will [
pany
ums
pop[
may
oper
fina[
sens
posi[

less efficient than the preceding one, even if it is perhaps more profitable, simply because it has discouraged good drivers from making an effort to drive well. Such, in essence, is Shleifer and Summers's proposed interpretation: the 1980s financial revolution created value because it repudiated a number of implicit contracts by dismissing older employees, by not renewing business with subcontractors, and by demanding that "managers" betray their past contracts with other stakeholders of the company. These actions may be efficient with regard to the stock value; they are also at times committed in defiance of economic efficiency.

This "breach of contract" signals the first act of the re-leveling of "managerial" capitalism. Throughout the 1980s, the trend was for the downsizing of companies. This signaled the end of Fordist production (which saw everything as big and roomy) and the entrance of lean production (which sees that products are customized). Raiders break up the huge conglomerates and sell their various subsidiaries piece by piece, subsequently re-centering their activities on the corporation's "core business."

The 1990s signaled the second act of the financial revolution. The time of disruption over, restoration was at hand. Hereafter concentrating on a single trade, companies began to grow prosperous again, merging with others that had the same core business. The logical aim was always cost reduction, but this time through large-scale application of intensive work principles. It was no longer a question of realizing scale economies in the old industrial sense. In the "flexible" world of the computer revolution, size is no longer the determining factor that it had been in the first days of serial production. Now at issue much more often in merging is the need to avoid all possible duplicate jobs by making one person do what two or three did formerly. In the future this will almost always be, an important motivation for mergers and dismissals.

At the beginning of these major reorganizations, the stock market was a crucial factor, at once a catalyst and an opportunist. It is an opportunist, as Shleifer and Summers showed, because the stock market repudiates implicit contracts connected to traditional company partners. It is a catalyst because huge mergers are made possible—most often by exchanging stocks, without obligating a company to draw heavily on its cash in order to effect a takeover. The raider is not "the man of écus," as Marx referred to the capitalist. The big stock battles bring in no capital in the general sense of the term—that is, in the sense of new resources that allow for financing various projects. Instead they carry with them other benefits: the opportunity to apply new organizational principles to labor and to be open to innovative technology. To speak in a formula, these battles depend in large part on the human capital of the firms of which they take possession. Intoxicated by the creation of "value," the stock market nonetheless generally reaches a point where this fundamental point of view is lost.

We can make judgments by following what happens *after* these mergers. As *The Economist* ruthlessly noted in an article titled "How to Merge: After the Deal,"[9] numerous unwelcome surprises await restructured firms. Two out of three times, the merger fails and the stock value of the firm that took the initiative to merge falls lower than it had been in the first place. One malicious economist even demonstrated that the subsequent fall was proportionate to how many times the firm's director had appeared on the covers of financial news magazines. The idea that a company can increase its value by means of restructuring and layoffs most often results from blindness to a simple but essential point: according to ordinary estimates, half of a firm's stock value comes from the human capital, and (only) the other half from actual capital. The importance of the human factor is systematically underestimated.

This is borne out by numerous examples.[10] When Sony and Matsushita bought Hollywood studios, they planned to integrate a natural production course: one that goes from film production to distribution to video sales. They discovered *a posteriori* that the synergies they "dreamed" of were only superficial, and that in practical terms making a film and showing it are two different things. Too late they understood that film producers have an "industry culture" which is totally incompatible with that of television manufacturers. As further examples we can examine the recent mergers undertaken with Internet companies. AOL, Netscape, and Sun Microsystems are allies in the development of e-commerce. Who can judge, though, where the alliance will end up? As *The Economist* writes, Netscape is still staffed with hackers (the idealistic computer pioneers) who still think in terms of a 1970s libertarian ideology. AOL is a mass service, more like Galeries Lafayette or Macy's than like students at Berkeley.

Beyond industrial errors, which are understandable in times as unsettled as these, there is an essential trait which is always underestimated by the stock raiders and which is crucial nonetheless: the exit from managerial capitalism (pronounced dead by the stock market) cannot be considered independently of the production transformations of which first Toyotaism and then computer science were the vectors. And all these transformations rested on a new image of work, signaling the entrance to a new period whose stakes are better understood in terms of human capital than in terms of financial capital.

The Era of Human Capital

In the image shared by Marxism and standard economic theory, work is generally interpreted as a "flux" rented by the firm either by day or by month, like a faucet that is turned on for 8 hours every day and whose energy flows into the pipes of the capital. We can say that labor had such a destiny under Taylorism. Even auteurs became anonymous strings of a framework that dictated their task. Today, however, we are witness to a return of the auteur. The worker must henceforth confer with clients or with colleagues and make decisions. The new model of production that took Fordism's place opened a horizon, or at least created the demand for one, where workers must

sition between shareholder values and stakeholder values, and at the methods of bypassing it.

Stakeholder Values

The difficulty of speaking about shareholder values in a positive (and not merely defensive) light has to do in part with the fact that it is nearly impossible to fix an analogous human capital criterion to the stock value of financial capital. The idea of adding a "social" index to the stock index is not realistic. The difficulty of obeying two masters aside, it is particularly delicate to set out explicit "governing" rules that correspond to the social well-being of a firm's partners or stakeholders.

There is, however, a comparison that clarifies the question. As Jean Tirole illustrates, a company's "government" is more than a little analogous to a regular government with respect to the quest for "social well-being."[13] Heads of government institutions would be at great pains to define their objectives explicitly by means of an index; nonetheless, they ordinarily know what they must do. It is the constraint of re-election that guides what they do. According to Popper, democracy is first of all the means by which the people can overturn bad governing parties at little cost. In the case of a company, the dissatisfied employees can strike, but this is very costly socially. They can leave, but at their own expense. How can new stakeholder values be invented in a way that does not contradict shareholder values?

In his report on European labor rights reform, Supiot proposed the exercise of a new idea that illustrates what this citizenship could well be. He suggested instituting a "Social Drawing Right" evoking the Special Drawing Rights invented in the 1960s to reform the international monetary system (and bearing the same acronym). The principle is to accord workers a right to a time saving account, allowing them to choose (within constraints) when they will take time off from work, whether for training, for vacation, for independent work, or for starting a company. This non-negotiable right would obligate the company to comply, since it would be claimed by the employee, much like today's maternity leaves, which oblige the firm to rehire the worker. It would oblige the company to integrate this "exit right" into its calculations to which the employee can make claim when he or she feels threatened.

The right to take a sabbatical as in the academic tradition is connected to remedies often proposed for combating the risk of mental fatigue carried by the new capitalism. Like sick leave, this right would limit companies' influence over employees' lives. But above all, it would serve as a preventive measure. The worker could decide when to make use of his or her social security rights. Today, social security provisions apply when a worker is sick or retires; the worker does not decide when these provisions can be activated.

By creating new rights, are we not further weighing down companies' already overflowing plates? We can answer this question with an example from the Netherlands, which activated a reform for part-time labor that appeared to harden its terms. When a firm offers a job to someone, it has no legal right to oppose the position's being accepted on a part-time basis (unless it can demonstrate that such a solution would put the firm in danger). In addition, once a part-time post has been granted, the firm cannot oppose its conversion to full-time (barring, again, legal demonstration that this solution is impossible for the company). This seemingly quite restrictive right actually *liberated* the part-time position, affording women (most often) the opportunity to seek jobs in workplaces that are not ghettos. Companies have also benefited, part-time work often being a way to adapt to constraints engendered by the "flexibility" of production. This is the same lesson we saw illustrated many, many times in the past century. In only considering labor rights as a cost, one is deprived of any possibility of creating a cooperative environment. Instead what is created is a "toxic" world, which is not the best way to place value on a firm's human capital at a time when the human role is becoming essential.

II   Can Capitalism
        Survive?

5   Sad Stories of the
Death of Kings

First there was the end of peasants, then of workers, and today what? The end of employees? The end of work in general? As the new industrial revolution unfolds, old questions arise. Like a saturnalian god devouring his children, each stage of capitalist development seems to devour the portion of civilization that engendered it. Agriculture, in which 80 percent of people had worked since the beginning of time, has seen an abrupt increase in its productivity. The price of agricultural products collapsed, farmers left the countryside, and the share of agricultural labor could not but fall. Then it was industry's turn to follow the same course. The time for a tertiarized economy subsequently arrived, with employees replacing laborers. Now that the computer revolution is subjecting services to a new productivity shock, doesn't the trap snap shut again? We lack a term to describe the next stage. What will happen if productivity continues to grow on its own, without outlets into which unemployed workers may "pour"?[1]

To understand the general logic of the switch from agriculture to industry and then to service, we must first return to the idea of services. In the end, what would an exclusively tertiary society mean? Would this be a society where the consumption of things remained essential, though no longer their production? Would their circulation (publicity) or their conception (creators, engineers) then account for the majority of employment? Or would society itself progressively saturate the consumption of objects, finally preferring yoga classes, or any other activity where the object share is put on a short allowance? The "tertiarization" of society is not helpful in answering this question. Too many heterogeneous dimensions are clustered in this idea.

We can get a clearer view by re-grouping activities according to criteria other than the standard ones. Let us make a single group of all activities that contribute to the production of material objects, or to the production of objects. In this large sector, we include production itself and any company consulting activities. What will we discover with the help of this aggregation?[2] An extraordinary stability in the course of the twentieth century! Indeed, the production of objects takes up a constant portion: 40 percent of the total employment in 1920 (both in France and the United States) and 40 percent in 1990 (again in France and the United States). "Service" activities show quite an increase in strength, but it is of no importance; these tasks are directly or indirectly connected to serving production.[3]

Beyond the production of objects, let us consider a second sector: intermediation. We include in this sector all commercialization activities and all activities that contribute to intermediating or mutualizing risks (e.g., banks and insurance companies). This sector also is remarkably stable; it represented 18.7 percent of American employment in 1920 and 20.7 percent in 1990. It began a bit lower in France (15 percent) but made up the difference in 1990 (20.5 percent). In the image of object production, intermediation scarcely evolves according to these statistics.

It is therefore among the "rest" of the economy that the great twentieth-century transformation has developed. This remainder comprises agriculture, education, and health care. At the beginning of the twentieth century, agriculture represented about three-fourths of this sector. At the end of the century, exactly the opposite was true. Agriculture had practically disappeared, and henceforth social services would constitute the majority of third-sector jobs.

There is quite a bit of flux in the job structure over the century, and its scope is clear. It is not a question of shortening the position of object production strictly speaking in the bulk of employment, but of substituting the *production of humans by land* (agriculture) with the *production of humans by human capital* (education and health). From now on, objects and humans can be said to be even; today they secure equal portions of the total labor force. Consequently, it is right to affirm that the portion of employment dedicated to objects has not changed, technological progress thus serving the growth of their production. It is equally right, however, to argue—like the end-of-work theorists—that human work seems to be returning to humans themselves.

The progressive "humanization" of production in the course of the century is at once well known (the twentieth century being that of Social Security) and mysterious. Should we not instead speak of "dehumanization" to understand the assembly line? One way to address this question is to make a detour through the theories that claim that technological progress make the worker useless. Through the fallacies of these theories, end-of-work theories shed light on this question.

End of Work?

Jeremy Rifkin wrote about the onset of the Information Age in his 1995 book *The End of Work,* noting how vast numbers of people, regardless of rank in the labor force, are being pushed toward unemployment lines or even soup kitchens by more and more sophisticated machines capable of doing an increasing number of previously human tasks.[4] In *The Human Condition,* Hannah Arendt spoke of the burden of work and the subservience of necessity.[5] According to Arendt, liberating humanity from this most ancient and most natural burden would open a forbidding epilogue: "the perspective of a society of workers with no work, the fact notwithstanding that it is possible to imagine worse things."

These gloomy predictions concerning the end of work are not new. At the turn of the nineteenth century, Sismonde de Sismondi expressed the fear that it would be possible one day for the king to execute all of England's production at the turn of a single crank.[6] This concern is among the millennial worries that ordinarily irritate economists. In their eyes, it is actually the contrary: technological progress is the ultimate source of growth, which is always good for employment. In fact, the idea that technological progress could be harmful to the employment rate can be refuted by examining the most basic criteria. In the course of the Trente Glorieuses (as the French called the post–World War II period of economic growth), labor became twice as productive, and unemployment had never been so low. Conversely, the increase of unemployment in the 1970s and the 1980s is usually interpreted by economists as an effect of the deceleration of technological progress, not its growth.

Let us nevertheless follow the radical perspective offered by Sismondi, who depicted a world where production takes place at zero cost. If products cost nothing, is it the "end of history," or at least the end of economic history? The general response from economists on this point is that no, other products will appear to feed consumers' minds. When the price of agricultural products decreased, industrial products rose, supplying new goods that farmers had never heard about. In turn, as industrial prices decrease, post-industrial products are miraculously generated. This aspect of the "materialistic" destiny of humanity is at work today in a very palpable way. The new consumer age is budding: the age of "channel surfing" and of post-modern custom-made consumption, which replaces the "what you see is what you get" mindset of the old mass consumption.

But this reveals only one side of the question. In order to see other facets, we should follow Sismondi's logic further—particularly his idea of *all* production's depending on the activation of one lever, not only the production of things we now consume but also that of all things imaginable in the future. Thus released from the "subservience of necessity," could we say that economic history will finally come to a conclusion? All the authors who either fear or applaud such an open view think as much, but this will in no way be the case. If and when all products are free, *man* will be expensive—infinitely so in this borderline case.

This is the point toward which we are heading, even though this is hard to admit in a world where so many human beings are still so poorly paid. For the industrialized countries, this is the tendency that explains the pressure that is exerted on labor. The fact that the value of human time becomes infinitely expensive with respect to the price of objects is not without consequences for the worker. In order to see why, it is instructive to read *Performing Arts: The Economic Dilemma*,[7] in which William Baumol and William Bowen analyze how the rising price of human time has changed the performing arts, not necessarily for the better.

That's Entertainment

The theatre is, it would seem, a world where technology is banished. Taking on a role, like playing an instrument, is an activity that has remained relatively unchanged for centuries. It takes Richard II just as much time today as yesterday to hear "sad stories of the death of kings."[8] The theatre remains essentially isolated from the "techno-logical" world, which contributes to its grandeur but also signals its downfall.

Because the theatre is cut off from the technological world, its costs are rising. This is to be expected in com-parison to such entertainments as the cinema or television, which have benefited from modern technological contri-butions, but it applies even more generally in comparison to other expenditures. It is much more costly today, for example, to go to the theatre than to buy a Bible, though in Shakespeare's time the opposite was true. Publishing has benefited from technological progress; the theatre has not. The fact that one rarely weighs reading the Bible against going to the theatre makes the comparison no less enlight-ening. Baumol and Bowen evince some astonishing data: In 1771, the Covent Garden Theatre had to earn £157 per production. In 1963, the Royal Shakespeare Theatre had to advance £2,139 per production, representing an increase nearly twice the average inflation rate. And still this estimate does not take into account the fact that the quality of these productions has declined perceptibly! When Shakespeare's works were first performed, there were on average 50 major plays produced per season and 25 "afterpieces" between seasons. The costumes, the number of actors, and the set designs were far more dazzling than those of today.

This same story is played out again and again in nearly all of the performing arts. With inflation taken into account, the New York Philharmonic Orchestra saw its prices multiply by five over the course of one century. Always present is what Baumol and Bowen refer to as a "cost disease," which makes it inexorably more expensive to produce ballets and operas. This explains why theatre attendance has gradually decreased since 1900 and why artists live so poorly. They frequently follow a second profession, most often as teachers, and their rank on the scale of revenue has difficulty even staying at middle level.

How is this possible? Don't technological progress and the increase in productivity allow everything to be cheaper than in Shakespeare's day? Isn't it easier now to light stages, sew costumes, and transport actors? Certainly, but these advances lead to the same result: *things* cost less and less, but humans become the most expensive commodity. Because it will hereafter be much more costly to hire actors, extras, or directors, or to pay rents indexed on residential rates and median salaries, everything seems much more expensive today in a sector, such as the theatre, where humans are the chief raw material.

If, as Marx or Ricardo thought, the only effect of technology would be to augment the volume of production, leaving workers' salaries unchanged, this cost disease would disappear. Hourly wages would remain constant, as would entertainment prices. But this is not the case. A French worker earned less than $2,000 a year in the middle of the nineteenth century; today a French worker makes more than $14,000 working only half as many hours. And actors do not live on a separate planet from other people. If other workers witness a raise in their salaries thanks to technological progress, it is inconceivable that actors would not be caught up in this gain. This necessarily raises performance prices.

Such was the last word of Baumol and Bowen at the time of their analysis, which provoked a palpable increase in public aid to the arts in the United States. The evolution was paralleled in France. As economic productivity doubled during the Trente Glorieuses, state aid to the performing arts increased. In 1960, 80 percent of the operating costs of the Comédie-Française came from receipts and 20 percent from subsidies. Today these proportions are exactly reversed: the theatre of Molière owes 80 percent of its revenue to government subsidies. Between 1960 and 1990, state aid to theatres more than quadrupled.

Still this has not hindered things from running their natural course. The intrusion of modern technology has been relentless, if not in the theatre then at least all around it. Through radio, motion pictures, television, videos, and the like, modern entertainment as a whole has sought to crack the technological scarcity of live performance, so that "sad stories of the death of kings" can be re-transmitted as many times as possible, ensuring that the salaries of the actors who pronounce the magical phrases will be based on the number of repeated broadcasts and permitting them to rejoin their peers in the circle of productivity.

The paradox of the actor can therefore be clarified this way: Why is a world in which machines are subjugated to humans so unfriendly to activities in which humans are the live resource? The answer is simple: Technology appears to eliminate humans, and indeed it does limit their usefulness. But this economic principle spreads because of the irresistible increase in the price of humans in comparison with objects. It is here that the most tragic misunderstanding of our age comes into play. When a future in which only humans have value is portrayed as the end of economic history, we are given to think that the economy will allow the completion of a truly human scheme in which activities such as flute playing and story telling will finally regain their rightful places. But this is not right, and this is where the disappointment comes from. Technology may well liberate humans from the subjugation of necessity, but humans will certainly not be free of technology itself.

6   The Island of the Unemployed

Schumpeter said that after times of prosperity there are often times of adaptation characterized by high unemployment, citing the periods 1820–1830, 1870–1880, and 1930–1940 as examples. To these we could add the years 1970–1980. With a regularity that will probably never be explained, capitalism alternates between crisis and prosperity "every fifty years."[1] It could be said that end-of-work theorists are mistaken in taking each of these crises as evidence that the end of work is near, rather than simply as a period of restructuring. Their reasoning is simple and at times takes on the appearance of fact. Blue-collar workers are needed, then are turned away; employment in manufacturing decreases, and unemployment increases accordingly. End-of-work theorists treat employment as a *difference* between companies' work "needs" (which are continually being reduced by technical progress) and the supply of workers looking for jobs (which therefore must be reduced artificially).

Modern unemployment theories, which feed the debate about economic policy objectives, treat unemployment not as a difference but as a *ratio* between the working population and the unemployed one. To grasp the stakes of this apparently semantic but fundamental distinction, imagine what would happen if a country's active population doubled from one day to the next. The unemployment *rate* would probably increase (at least at first), but it is unbelievable that the entire second half of the active population would join the ranks of the unemployed, waiting for jobs that must be shared between the two. The radical Malthusianism that rests on the hypothesis that there is a *fixed* number of jobs that nothing (not even the growth of the active population) could ever alter is obviously naive.

For most of the theories contributing to the analysis, "structural unemployment" is actually expressed by a balanced relationship between the number of those who have jobs and those who do not. The debate is over the rates themselves There is no consensus among economists on the "structural" unemployment rate. In France, an optimistic estimate would put it at about 6 or 7 percent; a more pessimistic estimate would place it at 9 or 10 percent. The optimists will plead for a more expansionary monetary or fiscal policy than the pessimists, who will be on their guard against the limits of such a policy and will campaign for structural reforms (the burden of expenses, company start-up costs, etc.). They all share the same fundamental idea, though: Unemployment is not determined "absolutely" by the mechanical difference between the manpower "needs" of companies and the people who need jobs; it is the result of a relationship between those who want to work, the active population, and the percentage of that population which can be absorbed by the system. In other words, unemployment is above all a relationship between those who have jobs and those do not. It is not an accounting difference.

The Ship of the Jobless

The simplest way to understand these concepts of unemployment is as follows: Much as Michel Foucault used to illustrate the advent of the classical age by telling the story of the ship of fools, imagine a ship that takes on board all the French jobless, then leaves them on a deserted island. If these 2 million people were representative of French society, they would include doctors, plumbers, teachers, and so on. How long would it take to construct a new economy on this island if the inhabitants were to sell their services to one another, transforming formerly unemployed people into active members of the insular society? The question is so speculative that it seems futile to try to answer. We can nonetheless support our hypothesis with the historic examples that most closely resemble our scenario.

After World War II, Japan and Germany were not far removed from our island of the unemployed: two countries completely destroyed by the war, with supernumerary manpower in relation to their remaining available facilities. And yet, in less than 10 years the miracle of reconstruction was perfectly evident. Growth was rapid, and the two economies had regained full employment.

How was such a "miracle" possible? In *The Rise and Decline of Nations*, Mancur Olson studies these two examples in detail.[2] Olson's theory, inspired by his earlier book *The Logic of Collective Action*, wants "new" or "destroyed" nations to be entirely occupied by the same collective project: reconstruction. From there, no real difficulty exists in finding the modalities of cooperative, collective action. How many hospitals and schools? What legal workday length? So many questions for which answers usually can be found quite easily. There is actually an immense difference between a country in "reconstruction" and a poor country, at least in terms of a developing country. In the case of postwar Germany, for example, society did not need to be invented, simply reconstituted. The way people cut their hair, care for themselves, educate their children, and so on—all this makes up the shared culture of the Germans. What is lacking is "only" infrastructure, equipment—in short, capital. But this is nothing in comparison to common knowledge. We estimate the total capital accumulated by an industrialized nation as equal to 3 years of production. (If we put its gross remuneration at 10 percent, we then find the part of the capital remuneration that corresponds to 30 percent of the annual wealth, which is the established amount.)

If we admit that capital is barely an obstacle (taking into account the flexibility of the financial market), and if we also admit that the unemployed would know—as in postwar Germany—how to provide themselves with common institutions propitious to reconstruction, nothing keeps us from imagining the island of the unemployed becoming a new El Dorado where nearly everyone finds a job. This is a valuable lesson. The idea that there would be unemployment due to technological progress causing a saturation of opportunities comes up against an absurdity: the unemployed themselves have needs, which are most often unsatisfied.

However, on the tack begun by this analogy, are we sure that the island of the unemployed forms a downsized version of France, where we would find hairdressers, doctors, and cobblers in identical proportions to the original? Of course not. Unemployed workers are in no way representative of French society. Half of them are recruited on an income scale that corresponds to the weakest fourth of French society. In other words, the unemployed actually make up a mini-society corresponding to the lowest echelon of the country and thus not at all representative of French society at large.

Could it be that this disproportion explains their joblessness in the first place? If one engineer is necessary for every ten workers and there is a shortage of the former, then the workers will never be employed. Such is Alfred Sauvy's theory.[3] Any gardener knows that a pipe through which no water flows is blocked at the narrowest point. It is because of a shortage of people whose positions entail little or no unemployment that there is unemployment at all. This idea is the starting point from which we explain unemployment of unskilled workers today. Pushed out of the factories, workers lacking the qualifications of the Fordist era suddenly found themselves too numerous in relation to society's relative needs. Here we touch upon an essential point in relation to which a certain Malthusianism can be justified. For example, by offering early retirement to former steelworkers, we spare them the bitter process of returning to work where they are redundant. Nonetheless, this idea fails completely when we apply it to the whole of society, since it can only act to correct a relative imbalance.

In this respect, the situation would be simpler on the island. Even unbalanced by the absence of doctors and an excess of former metalworkers, unemployment would end by adjusting abilities to needs and finding the road to "reconstruction." After all, Singapore's postwar population that was 75 percent illiterate, a fact that did not keep the country from finding the way to rapid growth and full employment. Admitting that it could be the same on the island of the jobless, let's look again at the question: What allows the unemployed to find jobs when they are separated from the rest of society but requires them to remain inactive when they are mixed with the society? The set of debates on the causes of unemployment can theoretically be found beneath this question.

The first explanation provided is that on the island the unemployed have no other recourse but to work, whereas life in French society offers other alternatives: for the young, to prolong their studies and live with their parents;

for women, to stay at home; for the elderly, to take early retirement. In fact, these three categories—the young, married women, and the elderly—are the ones in which unemployment is most severe. The explanation is short, however. Why are such differences observed from one country to the next in respect to these categories themselves? And why is there so much unemployment even among men between 30 and 50 years of age?

The second explanation opposes the one proposed by Mancur Olson to explain the successful reconstructions in Germany and Japan. Simply put, labor market regulations of various sorts do not work in favor of the jobless. For example, the minimum wage, licensing costs, hiring costs, and the expense of training new hires create an invisible barrier which the unemployed have difficulty turning to their advantage. Conversely, as soon as these people are put on our island, these institutions are immediately revised in a way that more appropriately fits the situation.

If we take this analysis even further, we rapidly discover that the institutions governing the job market, which are often held accountable for problems therein, actually represent only one aspect of the problem. Why would an unemployed hairdresser have difficulty setting up business in France while being able to create one on our island? The answer is simply that he or she is rid of competition from other hairdressers. A hairdresser set up on an island can seat his clients on a chair in the middle of the square if he likes; no French hairdresser could do that.

In effect, unemployed hairdressers are up against a "standard" implicitly fixed by others. *Regardless of the price of a haircut*, the unemployed themselves will quite often go to a hairdresser who is appropriately installed. Therefore, in a way that may seem insignificant, we see that a "developed" nation sets standards that make all the difference between employment on the island and employment at home. At home, who would lend money to a struggling hairdresser? On the island, where banks have no choice, funds would be much more abundant for those who would be considered bad risks back home. In this light, unemployment seems much more like one of the more tragic sides to poverty in rich countries, like a social relationship between those who have jobs and those who don't.

The Return Ship

Now let us bring the ship of the jobless back home. Is this imaginary exercise in integrating the unemployed vain? Not always.

In 1962, when Algeria became independent, 900,000 French colonials suddenly entered France.[4] The majority of them settled in the south, where economic conditions were not really the best. The Evian Agreements, promising Algerian independence, were signed in March of that year and approved by referendum in April. In May, the influx began in force. In job market percentage, immigrants were 1.6 percent of France's population. In some regions the ratio was much higher. In the department of Provence-

Côte-d'Azur, for example, immigrants made up 5.6 percent of the population.

With the arrival of the repatriates, France's unemployment rate doubled in a year. However, scarcely a year later it had returned to the previous level. After another 6 years, the economic situation in regions where the biggest numbers of repatriates had settled (Provence-Côte-d'Azur and Languedoc-Roussillon) was far from deteriorating in comparison with the rest of the country. Thus, between 1962 and 1968 the unemployment rates of these two regions rose at a pace that was just under the national average. In fact, as G. Tapinos notes,[5] the arrival of the Algerian nationals was a bonus for the regions welcoming them. Of course, not all the repatriates found their place in France. In 1968, their unemployment rates were more than twice the national average (4.5 percent versus 2.1 percent), and this ratio was repeated almost uniformly throughout the regions where they settled. But look at these statistics in light of our island of the unemployed: 95 percent of those who applied received jobs.

The Algerian example is not at all extraordinary. From 1989 on, nearly 500,000 Russians arrived in Israel, increasing the active Israeli population by about 12 percent.[6] This was a demographic shock six times bigger (in relative terms) than that of the repatriates from Algeria. Nonetheless, in 1995 the Israeli unemployment rate had returned to its pre-immigration level. Another example is the Portuguese *ritornados*. At the time of their independence, Africa's Portuguese colonies included Angola,

Mozambique, Cape Verde, Guinea-Bissau, and São Tomé and Príncipe. Six hundred thousand colonists, *ritornados*, returned to Portugal in less than 3 years. Added to this demographic shock was the one induced by the country's demilitarization, which loosed 200,000 soldiers onto the job market. At the same time, emigration suddenly stopped. In 1981, the *ritornado* unemployment rate was around 14 percent, against the active population's unemployment rate of 6 percent. An abrupt but convincing way to illustrate this analysis is to compare Portuguese unemployment to that of Spain or France. Portugal's unemployment rate is much lower than Spain's, and when the evolution of Portuguese unemployment is thus put into international perspective it is impossible to conclude that the *ritornados* had a negative effect on Portugal's jobless rate.

Enter the Baby Boomers

Before drawing lessons from these case studies, let us consider another example: the successful entrance of French baby boomers into the job market, and the relative setback for subsequent generations in finding a place for themselves in the 1990s.[7] For these generations born between 1940 and 1955, it is permissible to say that the Trente Glorieuses actually continued after the crisis of 1975. The salaries of this generation increased by 20 percent between 1975 and 1995. Their unemployment rate was 7 percent, versus 12.5 percent for the rest of the population. An even more radical index attests to the favorable situation of this generation: the suicide rate. People in their thirties now are twice as likely to commit suicide as in 1965; those in their fifties are 25 percent less likely to do so. For the first time in history, more people kill themselves at age 30 than at age 60. Indisputably, baby boomers profited more from the modern world than other generations.

Now compare the baby boomers' destiny with that of the following generation. Between 1987 and 1993, while the inflation-adjusted average salary of salaried employees as a whole increased by more than 10 percent, entry-level salaries decreased by 4 percent. More specifically, supported by the work of Christian Baudelot and Michel Gollac,[8] we can take a detailed look at the position of a sample group: thirty-something workers. How does being 30 in 1977 compare with being 30 today? We see first of all that their salaries decreased continuously, going from $17,600 to $16,400 between 1977 and 1985, then to $16,000 in 1993. During the Trente Glorieuses, young people entered the job market with a salary which was always superior to that of their elders when they first started their careers. Such is no longer the case. Moreover, if we measure the difference in incomes between father and son in the course of the same year, the gap widens considerably. In 1964, the monthly income of a 50-year-old father exceeded that of his 25-year-old son by only $250; in 1993 this difference had grown to more than $800.

How can we account for such a change? The most natural explanation reverts back to the end of the Trente Glorieuses. The mechanical effect of rapid postwar growth clearly illustrates why a young person always earned more than his father when the latter began his career. However, it does not allow us to understand the reasons for the gap created, at a given time, between the salaries of father and son. Why doesn't the economic slowdown make its mark on everyone uniformly, simultaneously reducing the salaries of both generations?

To answer this question, it is necessary to return to the levels of education of the various cohorts. The baby boomers who arrived on the job market reduced the gap between them and their parents by the fact of their diplomas. In 1970, 20 percent of French people in their thirties had their "bac" (baccalaureate—the high school certificate, for which one takes an examination at age 17 or 18), while only 13 percent of salaried employees had theirs. Today, 30 percent of people in their thirties are bac holders, but 25 percent of those in their fifties are. Though the young have more diplomas than their elders, they no longer have the same *relative* advantage as in the past. The first baby boomers who appeared on the job market could compensate for their lack of experience with more study. This was not the case with subsequent generations; they are not significantly more educated than their elders. The "Open sesame!" of diplomas works only for the first generation that uses it.

This explanation provides a key for understanding why the drawbridge lowered for the baby boomers but not for subsequent generations. But this answer does not help us understand the *fall* of the *absolute* level of remunerations of

market. Malthusianism, which invariably proposes resolving crises confronting society by decreasing the number of its members, is one of the two great ideological temptations of our age for which Europe, with its mass unemployment, was the breeding ground. Increased duration of education, early retirement, and reduction of work time are just so many manifestations of the attraction of this ideology, which repeats the errors of the usual end-of-work reasoning.

Malthusianism commits the mistake of confusing the crisis years experienced in industrialized economies since the 1960s with a permanent new employment regime. It is one thing to offer pre-retirement options to metalworkers whose factories have shut down; it is another thing to establish in government the precept that the best response to the destruction of jobs is the disappearance of jobs. By being blind to this conclusion, Malthusianism offers the model of a closed society. As is shown by Algerian repatriates and by the *ritornados*, the key to fighting unemployment lies in an open society.

7 Can Capitalism Survive?

The modern laborer, . . . instead of rising with the progress of industry, sinks deeper and deeper below the conditions of existence of his own class. He becomes a pauper, and pauperism develops more rapidly than population or wealth. And here it becomes evident, that the bourgeoisie is unfit any longer to be the ruling class in society, and to impose its conditions of existence upon society as an overriding law. It is unfit to rule because it is incompetent to assure an existence to its slave within his slavery, because it cannot help letting him sink into such a state, that it has to feed him, instead of being fed by him.[1]

These remarks from Marx touch upon the diagnosis of the end-of-work theorists: Capitalism shrinks the circle of those who can work and inexorably condemns most of them to misery. In a striking way, they resonate with the new rise in poverty and exclusion and exert a gripping seductive power over all who are concerned about where the modern world is drifting.

Start with the essentials: We do not understand capitalism if it is interpreted as a machine to "impoverish the masses." It is quite the contrary; everything about it is made to enrich the masses. As Schumpeter says, "the capitalist engine is first and last an engine of mass production, which unavoidably means also production for the masses." Schumpeter's illustration is eloquent enough to be quoted in full:

There are no doubt some things available to the modern workman that Louis XIV himself would have been delighted to have yet was unable to have—modern dentistry for instance. On the whole, however, a budget on that level had little that really mattered to gain from capitalist achievement. Even speed of traveling may be assumed to have been a minor consideration for so very dignified a gentleman. Electric lighting is no great boon to anyone who has money enough to buy a sufficient number of candles and to pay servants to attend to them. It is the cheap cloth, the cheap cotton and rayon fabric, boots, motorcars and so on that are the typical achievements of capitalist production, and not as a rule improvements that would mean much to the rich man. Queen Elizabeth owned silk stockings. The capitalist achievement does not typically consist in providing more silk stockings for queens but in bringing them within the reach of factory girls in return for steadily decreasing amounts of effort.[2]

These impressionistic matters can be found again in very similar terms in a classic work on the subject, Nathan Rosenberg and L. E. Birdzell's *How the West Grew Rich*. Rosenberg and Birdzell note that in most societies preceding capitalism, new products contributed to the happiness of the rich much more often than to that of the poor. One of the particularities of Western growth, conversely, is to have profited the poor more than the rich:

Innovations that reduced the cost of producing goods did not appreciably change the life-style of people who were abundantly able to pay pre-innovation prices, and the most lucrative new products were those with a market among the many, rather than among the few. Thus the first textile factories produced fabrics of inferior quality, which the rich did not want, and, a century later, the great automobile fortune was Henry Ford's not Henry Royce's. . . . It is much easier to think of innovations which benefited only the less well-off than it is to think of innovations which have benefited only the rich, and, in fact, the innovations of positive value to the rich are relatively few: advances in medical care, air conditioning, and improvements in transportation and preservation of food.[3]

And Rosenberg and Birdzell urge us to guard against the temptation of nostalgia:

If we take the long view of human history and judge the economic lives of our ancestors by modern standards, it is a story of almost unrelieved wretchedness. The typical human society has given only a small number of people a humane existence, while the great majority have lived in abysmal squalor. We are led to forget the dominating misery of other times in part by the grace of literature, poetry, romance and legend, which celebrate those who lived well and forget those who lived in the silence of poverty. The eras of misery have been mythologized and may even be remembered as golden ages of pastoral simplicity. They were not. . . .

The move from poverty to wealth is a move toward literacy, education, and a variety of experience. A life of poverty is a life in which survival is the first and almost the only order of business, in which housing is so crowded as to make privacy unknown, and in which choices are narrowly restricted. The move to wealth is a move toward greater possibilities of privacy and individual choice.[4]

Paradoxes of Capitalism

Maintaining these opinions at a time when capitalism is offering more reasons to be detested is obviously as delicate as, according to Schumpeter again, trying to convince an early Christian to see the merits of the previous civilization. But this is precisely the question: Why would capitalism, when everything points to its being the source of happiness for humanity, seem to be the source of unhappiness for individuals? How transitory are the miseries Marx said were the only logical outlet of the system?

Let us begin with the Marxian vision of work—a largely Hegelian vision heavily inspired by the work of the slave. Obviously Marx doesn't mean that the proletariat should be bought and sold like slaves; they rent their services, they are not sold. But like the slave, the worker owes everything to the master (the capitalist) for the duration of the rental of his or her work energies. At what price, or rather at what wage, is this rental carried out? Marx answered with a calculation that the owner of a slave would make. The worker's price would equal the expenditures of his care and upkeep; that is, one must pay to nourish and clothe a worker, even pay a little more if the master is generous. All this would be good business for the capitalist. Certainly the capitalist feeds the proletariat-slave, but the latter will work (well) beyond the time necessary to offset the expenses of his upkeep. Marx's entire theory is built on this reasoning, which is false in history's view. The worker's salary is indexed on wealth produced through his work, not on wealth necessary to his survival. Where does Marx's reasoning get caught? He commits the same sin made by those who defend the end-of-work theories: He is completely mistaken about the scope of the machine age and, perhaps more grave, about the nature of work.

The analogy of slave work helps us grasp the problem. The most frequent reference as far as this is concerned is from the *Politics*, where Aristotle justifies work by slaves with this famous formula: "For if every instrument could accomplish its own work [and] if, in like manner, the shuttle would weave . . . chief workmen would not want servants, nor masters slaves."[5] For Marx, as for the end-of-work theorists, the key to the modern machine age is contained in this quotation. The machine has no functions other than accomplishing Aristotle's prediction: replacing the work of modern slaves, the proletariat, by the work of automatons. But instead of making each person a "master" who is therefore freed of the weight of necessity, machinism deprives the proletariat of the means of survival, "transforming the poor into indigent" and thus permitting capitalists to oblige members of the proletariat to accept a wage of "misery," one which would permit them just to survive, like slaves. By another route, this issue parallels Hannah Arendt's prediction: Capitalism, under the reign of automation, creates "a society of laborers without labor, that is, without the only activity left to them; nothing could be worse."[6]

The paradox that is difficult to grasp at first glance is that a technology which reduces the content of work most often means that the work of whoever activates it will be more productive, which precisely allows a worker to earn more. Machinism has not allowed machines to actually take the place of humans; it offers them the chance to do more things thanks to the machine. We saw that this was indeed the case with the assembly line. Thanks to Fordism, the masses of unskilled workers at the factory gates at the dawn of the twentieth century could enter and increase their productivity. Such is the situation that is being produced by the computer today: It permits its user to do the work of several people and thus to augment his or her productive energy. This is the fundamental reason why salaries can, without contradiction, increase in step with technological progress: The latter is principally a means of increasing the productive capacity of workers, not reducing it as Aristotle imagined with the slaves.

Of course the question remains of how to pass this theoretical indexation of a worker's salary to the actual indexation of wealth produced. The fact that machines render workers more productive does not in itself obligate bosses to increase workers' salaries. The question of "full employment" comes into play here. While there is unemployment, bosses can commit blackmail by hiring another worker in the place of one who wants a raise. If the workers wanted "everything," there would necessarily be underemployment, since in that case it would be better to fire than to hire. But what happens if the workers claim only two-thirds of the produced wealth, which is approximately the observed figure? Some bosses will want more, as Ford did in his day. In paying workers better than competing firms, a company will get a good deal. Competition between capitalists is the instrument by which workers will get their "due"—that is, not the amount that allows them to survive, but the amount that really represents their contribution to production. Marx underestimated this dimension of capitalist competition.

Creative Destructions

If everything is rosy, why all the tears? Why is capitalism met with so much hostility? The answer doesn't take long to find. Capitalism leaves in its wake the destinies of those who were suddenly made useless by technological progress. For example, Aristotle dreamed that the "shuttle would weave . . . without a hand to guide" it, but in 1733, when an Englishman named John Kay invented a "flying shuttle" that increased cloth output he was chased out of Colchester and then pursued from town to town by rioters who well understand that the shuttle would take "their" jobs.

Let us follow the history begun by John Kay, which is perfectly representative of capitalism's own history. Kay's "flying shuttle" increase the efficiency of cloth manufacture by 20–30 percent. Although Kay had to flee, his technique was put into general use in the region. Very soon, a major imbalance manifested itself. With the weaving industry taking off, textile mills—most notably cotton mills—could not meet the new demand. This "bottleneck" threatened the development of the field in general. Weaving prices increased. Delivery delays increased and in turn held up the implementation of new looms. It was not until 1764 that another inventor, James Hargraves, perfected the "spinning jenny," which reduced the gear ratio of the old spinning wheel and would be equipped, down the road, with up to 100 spindles. The new machine was soon confronted with the fact that it depended entirely on human power. To remedy that shortcoming, Richard Arkwright invented the water frame, which first needed to be activated by hydraulic energy or by a team of horses. But these energy sources presented further challenges. In 1777, Arkwright appealed to James Watt to help improve the power source for the looms, and thus began the history of the steam engine.[8]

The textile industry encountered new bottlenecks in drapery bleaching. Formerly, fabrics were bleached with curdled milk and then by drying them in the sun. This called for lots of meadows and lots of cows. The entire chemical industry went to work to resolve this dysfunction. In 1774 isolated chlorine became the base for the bleaching. Sulfuric acid and soda subsequently became the principal ingredients, in turn generating further research. But white is one thing, color another. The race to manufacture colorants became the big issue in the nineteenth century. The first synthetic dye, commercialized in 1856, was due to an English chemist named W. H. Perkin. It permitted Queen Victoria to sport a superb mauve at the 1862 Exposition, arousing the ambition of all European chemists. The German chemical industry was born from this challenge, and in 1869 it was in Germany that the synthesis of alizarin was accomplished. Alizarin took the place of madder, grown in the Vaucluse, as the basis of red dyes. Thanks to the exceptional profits that followed, the Germans redoubled their efforts, uniting for the first time in history "theoretical" research and research for profit, even to the point of finding the Grail: the synthesis of indigo, which would be commercialized in 1901. On the way, the Germans invented aspirin in 1899, which led them toward participation in the modern pharmaceutical industry.

This result is far from the difficult beginnings of John Kay, but the course of research he created allows us to sketch the logic of industrial revolutions. Progress in one sector creates an imbalance among those productive processes that remain prisoner to old techniques. Their rise in costs irresistibly increases the pressure to innovate, which is resolved, transformed, and then carries further, to new sectors, the weight of the adjustment. As François Caron summarizes: "No technical system is exempt from dysfunction. When the compromises put in place to allow for system management become more and more difficult to negotiate, then an industrial revolution is necessary."[9] This growth is actually ordinary, and the imbalance is invariably the rule. It is like a balloon, where certain parts are less inflated than the rest, before swelling in turn and letting other protuberances appear. The principle is still the same. The growth race pushes the slower sectors to the breaking point and provokes innovations which at times take an autonomous route (from the dye industry is born the pharmaceutical industry, and so on).

We will never take full measure of the effects of technological progress if we do not evaluate the cause. Innovations are never created in a vacuum; they satisfy social needs, and they resolve tensions that had blocked the pursuit of growth. Curdled milk was replaced by solvents because it blocked the progression of the entire textile industry. But the fact that the number of curdled milk agents decreases in no way foreshadows the number of workers employed in the textile field. The progress in one sector liberates the productive forces of another. This is why we searched in vain for a global relationship between technological progress and unemployment, and this is why the notion of "technological unemployment" was never empirically established.[10]

From Slave to Modern Man

Generalizing what we saw in the textile field to the economy as a whole, Schumpeter described capitalism as a process of creative destruction constantly revolutionizing the economic structure from the inside while continually destroying its older elements and continually creating new ones. What his analysis nonetheless leaves out in the cold is the logic that allows for the understanding of these creative destructions. What is the axis? Opposing the new and the old is useful, but it is not very informative about what is to become of capitalist societies. The logic of industrial revolutions which we sketched from the textile field offers an essential key to a reading of this technological progress: It finds solutions to the shortages that hinder the course of growth every time. How can we interpret *our* contemporary modern times in this case? What shortages will our capitalism allow to be remedied? The answer that is suggested by the crisis of the Fordist economy can be phrased as follows: Modern capitalism had to address the shortage of individuals who wanted to work on the assembly line. The tears of that young woman in *Mai 1968* who refuses to return to the Wonder factory signal the death warrant of the assembly line, the best sign that it is necessary to move on to something else. The most flagrant cases where machines take a human's place purely and simply is when the work in question itself was rejected. In other cases, machines afford their users the opportunity to do more in less time: they offer ways to make one's work more productive.[11]

We can try to draw a parallel between the age in which we live and what economists have called the "demographic transition": the period (mostly in the nineteenth century) during which people suddenly decided to have fewer children and to take better care of those they already had. How can this transition be explained? Gary Becker sees here an *effect* of the new prosperity of industrial nations.[12] When a society becomes richer, it generally becomes less interested in quantity and more interested in quality. For example, we can use similar terms to interpret

the new world in which we live: The passage from the
reign of mass production's brute quantity to one of more
qualitative diversity becomes possible when a society has
become richer. Applied to demographics, this transition
would explain why we prefer having few children of
whom we take better care than many who would largely
be left to their own resources.

This thesis is interesting, but it contradicts the way his-
torians broach the question. They readily agree that for
children "qualitative" interest is a phenomenon that is
tardy in joining human history. For a long time, as
Philippe Ariès has shown,[13] children had been treated as
little adults and had wandered around among adults and
animals until able to take their turn at work. From the sev-
enteenth century on (*before* the industrial revolution), children experienced a change in status: They were given
children's clothes, and adults began to look after their
education. We must not say, therefore, that the "demographic transition" was a consequence of capitalism. It
would be more correct to say that capitalism gave the
transition the means to express itself.

Going back to the evolution of work in our modern
times, we can equally show that the departure from the
assembly line was not produced by a strictly economic
logic. The era of human capital we are entering was not
"desired" by capitalism. It is much more an effect of
democracy. Children entered school in the French
Republic at the beginning of the twentieth century at the
same moment when factories were designed to welcome

Conclusion

To the question "Can capitalism survive?" Schumpeter answered No, adding that this was not because capitalism would be devoured by internal contradictions but because its very success would render it detestable. Are capitalism's overly materialistic values bound to be disliked? Max Weber provides a fascinating answer:

> The notion that our rationalistic and capitalistic age is characterized by a stronger economic interest than other periods is childish; the moving spirits of modern capitalism are not possessed of a stronger economic impulse than for example, an oriental trader. The unchanging of the economic interest merely as such has produced only irrational results; such men as Cortez and Pizzarro, who were perhaps its strongest embodiment, were far from having an idea of a rationalistic economic life.[1]

If a "cultural" explanation for hostility toward capitalism were necessary, it would have to be sought not on the side of vice but on the side of virtue. What is often detested in capitalist society is, indeed, its pretension in wanting to rationalize everything, to want to do everything for the best, its "utilitarianism." Because capitalist civilization is rationalistic, it is also "anti-heroic" (as Schumpeter said), and it always needs exterior reinforcements to fulfill the portion of heroism demanded by human destinies. We can of course criticize capitalism's utilitarianism in the name of chivalrous enthusiasm, but we cannot deny it.

To the question why "our own modern times" sometimes seem harsher than the preceding ones, we can give two answers. The first is that our modern era is still an incomplete revolution. It lacks specific social regulation. The modern times of the past century had already known such a transitional phase in the course of which totalitarian temptation seemed irresistible, at the time playing the role held today by neo-liberalism. Inasmuch as a new set of social rules specific to our age will not have been found, unrest will remain. As long as the influence of financial capital eclipses the importance of human capital, the dissonance between private and public consumption will persist, and modern men and women will experience as a new "calvary" the entry into this new age of his history.

The second explanation of the contemporary malaise is of another, perhaps more profound, nature. Modern men and women are liberated from the subservience of necessity in many domains. Nonetheless, like the walker trying to reach the horizon, they are discovering that the end of the route remains just as far in the distance as ever. They understand that their work is endless. In part, they are victims of their own social fantasies, which want them always to outdo their neighbors. But it has always been thus, and this is not the heart of the question. Health care, education, and sports are no less worthy consumables than cars or washing machines. Contemporary humans are discovering more fundamentally that, even if the technological world progressively liberates them from necessity, it does not liberate them from technology itself. Like an actor who can no longer play a role in *Romeo and Juliet* without being exposed to the competition of greater artists who have recorded the play for television, modern people discover that in becoming richer they do not return to an original "pastoral simplicity." Each stage cleared with the help of technology demands that they make a greater effort to master that technology. Each step in prosperity adds more weight to the reasons they give to justify their place in society.

Notes

Introduction

1. François Caron, *Les Deux Révolutions industrielles du XXe siècle* (Paris: Albin Michel, 1997).

2. Philippe Askenazy, Organizational and Technological Innovations, Globalization and Inequalities, PhD thesis, Ecole des Hautes Etudes en Sciences Sociales, 1999.

3. "Nathan Rothschild died probably of staphylococcus or streptococcus septicemia. . . . This was before the germ theory existed, hence before any notion of the importance of cleanness. . . . And so the man who could buy anything died, of a routine infection easily cured today for anyone who could find his way to a doctor or hospital, even a pharmacy." David Landes, *The Wealth and Poverty of Nations* (New York: Norton, 1998), p. xviii.

4. Jean-Paul Sartre, *No Exit* (New York: Vintage, 1956).

Chapter 1

1. Aldous Huxley, *Brave New World* (New York: Perennial Classics, 1998), pp. 29, 52.

2. Edgar Morin, *Les Stars* (Paris: Seuil), cited in Jacqueline Nacache, *Le Film hollywoodien classique* (Paris: Nathan, 1995). See also C. A. Michalet, *Le Drôle de drame du cinema mondial* (Paris: Presses universitaires de

France); Francesco Casetti, *Les Théories du cinéma depuis 1945* (Paris: Nathan, 1999).

3. Nacache, *Le Film hollywoodien classique*.

4. Georges Friedmann, *Où va le travail humain?* (Paris: Gallimard, 1963). See also Stanley Parker, *The Future of Work and Leisure* (New York: Praeger, 1971).

5. Jacques Curie and Raymond Dupuy (citing Braudel), "L'Organisation du travail contre l'unité du travailleur," *Les histoires de la psychologie du travail*, ed. Y. Clot (Paris: Octares, 1996).

6. Karl Marx, *Capital: A Critique of Political Economy*, volume 1, ed. F. Engels (New York: International Publishers, 1967), p. 247.

7. Vauban, *La Dîme royale*, cited in Jean Fourastié, *Machinisme et bien-être* (Paris: Presses universitaires de France).

8. Cited in François Caron, *Les Deux Révolutions industrielles du XXe siècle* (Paris: Albin Michel, 1997).

9. Benjamin Coriat, *L'Atelier et le Chronomêtre* (Paris: Christian Bougois, 1979).

10. Friedmann, *Où va le travail humain?*

11. Daniel Bell, *Cultural Contradictions of Capitalism*, cited in Henri Weber, *Que reste-t-il de Mai 1968?* (Paris: Seuil, 1988; Points-Seuil, 1998).

12. Cited in J. P. LeGoff, *Mai 1968, l'héritage impossible* (Paris: La Découverte, 1998).

13. Michel Foucault, *The Order of Things* (New York: Pantheon, 1970), p. 387.

14. See also Weber, *Que reste-t-il de Mai 1968?* (where this is the central issue).

15. LeGoff, *Mai 1968*.

16. Antoine de Baecque, *La Nouvelle Vague, portrait d'une jeunesse* (Paris: Flammarion, 1998).

17. Ibid.

18. Nacache, *Le Film hollywoodien classique*.

Chapter 6

1. Joseph Schumpeter, *Business Cycles* (New York: McGraw-Hill, 1939).

2. Mancur Olson, *The Rise and Decline of Nations* (New Haven: Yale University Press, 1982).

3. Sauvy, *La Machine et le Diable*.

4. See Jennifer Hunt, "The Impact of the 1962 Repatriates from Algeria on the French Labor Market," *Industrial and Labor Relations Review* 45, no. 3 (April 1992), p. 556.

5. Cited in ibid., p. 558

6. Rachel Friedberg, The Impact of Mass Migration on the Israeli Labor Market, Working Paper 96-28, Brown University, 1996, p. 1.

7. See Louis Chauvel, *Le Destin des générations* (Paris: Presses Universitaires de France, 1998).

8. Christian Baudelot and Michel Gollac, "Le Salaire des trentenaires," *Economie et Statistiques* 301 (1997): 3–13.

9. Les Créations d'emplois en France et aux Etats-Unis, Notes de la Fondation Saint-Simon, December 1997.

10. See Denis Olivennes, Le Modèle social français, un compromis malthusien, Notes de la Fondation Saint-Simon, December 1998.

Chapter 7

1. Karl Marx, *The Communist Manifesto*, ed. F. Bender (New York: Norton, 1988), p. 66.

2. Schumpeter, *Capitalism, Socialism, and Democracy*, p. 67.

3. Nathan Rosenberg and L. E. Birdzell Jr., *How the West Grew Rich: The Economic Transformation of the Industrial World* (New York: Basic Books, 1986), p. 27.

4. Ibid., pp. 3–4.

5. Aristotle, *The Politics* (Cambridge University Press, 1988), p. 5.

6. Arendt, *The Human Condition*, p. 5

7. Cited in Sauvy, *La Machine et la Diable*.

8. See Patrick Verley, *La Révolution industrielle* (Paris: Gallimard, 1997); François Caron, *Le Résistible déclin des sociétés industrielles* (Paris: Perrin, 1985).

9. Cited in Caron, *Les Deux Révolutions industrielles du XXe siècle*.

10. Numerous studies have actually tried to quantify "technological unemployment" (that is, the portion of unemployment that is linked to technological innovations, in that they force workers to leave one profession to find another). Their balance sheet is not at all ambiguous: technological unemployment does not exist, or at least has very little influence. The most convincing study on this subject (Steven J. Davis, John C. Haltiwanger, and Scott Schuh, *Job Creation and Destruction*, MIT Press, 1996) shows that the essential part of this crossgame of job creation and destruction usually occurs within the same sector. Of course the loss of jobs due to technological innovations does exist. However this is but one tear in an ocean of reasons why workers lose jobs, most of which have to do with an overall economic situation or with the "ordinary" play between openings and closings of rival companies. On this subject, see R. Hall and D. Lillien, "Cyclical Fluctuations in the Labor Market," in *Handbook of Labor Economics* (North-Holland, 1986).

11. For a similar idea, see Daron Acemoglu, "Why Do New Technologies Complement Skills? Directed Technical Change and Inequality," *Quarterly Journal of Economics*, November 1998, pp. 1055–1089.

12. Gary Becker, *A Treatise on the Family* (Cambridge: Harvard University Press, 1981).

13. Philippe Ariès, *L'enfant et la vie familiale sous l'Ancien Regime* (Paris: Seuil, 1973).

Conclusion

1. Max Weber, *The Interpretation of Social Reality*, ed. J. Eldridge (London: Michael Joseph, 1971), p. 280.

Index

4. Robert Castel, *Les métamorphoses de la Question Sociale* (Paris: Fayard, 1995).

5. Ibid.

6. Gérard Abramovici, "La consommation des ménages depuis 1959" (*Données sociales*, INSEE, 1996).

7. It should equally be noted that a laborer who has more money becomes more a "rich laborer" than an executive, at least for the first generation. On this important point, which I will now put aside, see Baudelot and Establet, *Maurice Halwachs* (Paris: Presses Universitaires de France, 1994).

8. Rochefort, *La Société des consommateurs*.

9. Irène Théry, *Le Démariage* (Paris: Odile Jacob, 1993).

Chapter 4

1. See, for example, R. J. Overy, *The Nazi Economic Recovery, 1932–1938* (London: Macmillan, 1982).

2. John Kenneth Galbraith, *The New Industrial State* (Boston: Houghton Mifflin, 1967), p. 2.

3. Joseph A. Schumpeter, *Capitalism, Socialism and Democracy* (New York: Harper Torchbooks, 1942), p. 61.

4. Michel Aglietta, Le Capitalisme de demain, Notes de la Fondation Saint-Simon, November 1998.

5. For a synthesis, see Tirole, *The Theory of Industrial Organization*.

6. Oliver Williamson, *The Economic Institutions of Capitalism* (New York: Free Press, 1985).

7. Philippe D'Iribarne et al., *Culture et mondialisation* (Paris: Seuil, 1998).

8. Andrei Shleifer and Lawrence Summers, "Breach of Trust in Hostile Takeovers," in *Corporate Takeovers: Causes and Consequences*, ed. A. Auerbach (University of Chicago Press, 1988).

9. *The Economist*, January 9, 1999, pp. 21–23.

10. Ibid.

11. Gary Becker, *Human Capital*, third edition (University of Chicago Press, 1993). (Becker does not actually consider the last of these three types; I am borrowing here from Jean-Louis. Beffa, Robert Boyer, and Roger Touffut, Les Relations salariales en France, Notes de la Fondation Saint-Simon, June 1999.

12. Alain Supiot, *Au-delà de l'emploi* (Paris: Flammarion, 1999).

13. Jean Tirole, *Corporate Governance*, Université de Toulouse.

Chapter 5

1. Sauvy, *La Machine et le Diable*.

2. Here I rely upon the tables that appear on pages 324 and 330 of Castells, *Rise of the Network Society*.

3. Nevertheless, as Jean Gadrey illustrates in "La galaxie des services" (in *Le Monde du travail* ed. J. Kergouat et al., Paris: La Découverte, 1998), it is not necessarily a question of externalization of tasks (which results when the accountant of an industrial firm leaves and sets to work on his account.) The issue is activities which often develop internally and externally (tasks related to computerization, for example).

4. Jeremy Rifkin, *The End of Work: The Decline of the Global Labor Force and the Dawn of the Post-Market Era* (New York: Putnam, 1995).

5. Hannah Arendt, *The Human Condition* (University of Chicago Press, 1958), p. 5. See also Dominique Meda, *Le Travail: une valeur en voie de disparition* (Paris: Aubier, 1997).

6. Sismondi, *Economie politique*, cited in Alfred Sauvy, *La Machine et le Diable* (Paris: Dunod, 1980).

7. William Baumol and William Bowen, *Performing Arts: The Economic Dilemma* (New York: Twentieth Century Fund, 1966). Several studies were subsequently published; for a synthesis, see Françoise Benhamou, *L'Economie de la culture* (Paris: La Découverte, 1996).

8. Shakespeare, *Richard II*, act 3, scene 2, line 156.

9. In fact, John Lee spoke of the "instant and unquestioning obedience of men eager not to lose their five dollar day."

10. The theorists of industrial organization, and with them economic theory as a whole, are in turn convinced of the capital importance of thus distinguishing "observable" economic variables from those which are not observable or are only indirectly so. For the foundation of the new theory of industrial organization, see Jean Tirole, *The Theory of Industrial Organization* (MIT Press, 1988); for the economic foundations of information theory, see Jean-Jacques Laffont, *Cours de théorie micro-économique* (Paris: Economica, 1982).

11. C. Shapiro and J. Stiglitz, "Efficiency Wage as a Worker Discipline Device," *American Economic Review* 74 (1984), pp. 433–444.

12. "Where wages are high accordingly, we shall always find the work-men more active, diligent and expeditious than when they are low." (Smith, *Wealth of Nations*, p. 99)

13. Masahiko Aoki, *Information, Incentives and Bargaining in the Japanese Economy* (Cambridge University Press, 1988), p. 10.

14. *La Nouvelle Condition ouvrière*, Notes de la Fondation Saint-Simon, October 1998.

15. Askenazy, Innovations technologiques.

16. Alain Ehrenberg, *La Fatigue d'être soi* (Paris: Odile Jacob). According to certain estimates given in the book, nearly 50% of mental illnesses today have to do with "depression," 30% to neuroses, and 20% to psychoses.

17. "L'évolution de l'organisation du travail," in *Le Monde du travail*.

Chapter 3

1. Mark Twain, *Collected Tales, Sketches, Speeches, & Essays*, volume 2: 1891–1910 (New York: Library of America, 1992), p. 942.

2. Robert Rochefort, *La Société des consommateurs* (Paris: Odile Jacob, 1995).

3. Alfred Sauvy, *La Machine et le Diable* (Paris: Dunod, 1980).

19. Manuel Castells, *The Rise of the Network Society* (Oxford: Blackwell, 1996).

20. To again take Manuel Castells's formula.

21. Unix is a computer operating system developed by Bell Laboratories. While the Federal Communications Commission investigated the Bell System's monopoly, Bell Labs released Unix to the public. From that point on, academics pursued its development.

Chapter 2

1. Sources of the examples in this paragraph: Assar Lindbeck and Dennis Snower, Multi-Task Learning and the Reorganization of Work, IZA Discussion Paper, 1999; Robert Rochefort, *Le Consommateur-Entrepreneur* (Paris: Odile Jacob, 1997).

2. Adam Smith, *An Inquiry into the Nature and Causes of the Wealth of Nations* (Indianapolis: Liberty Fund, 1981), pp. 14–15.

3. Gary S. Becker and Kevin M. Murphy, "Specialization and Coordination," *Quarterly Journal of Economics* 107 (1992): 1137–1160.

4. This section is derived in large part from Philippe Askenazy's PhD thesis, Innovations technologiques et industrielles, internationalization et inégalités (Ecole des Hautes Etudes en Sciences Sociales, Paris, 1999) and from my fruitful discussions with Askenazy.

5. Michel Gollac, "Différences ou divisions? La diversité des métiers ouvriers," in *Le Monde du travail* (Edition la découverte "textes à l'appui," 1998).

6. Askenazy, Innovations technologiques et industrielles, internationalization et inégalités.

7. See Michel Gollac, "La Diffusion de l'informatique au travail," in *Données sociales* (INSEE, 1993).

8. See "Les histoires de la psychopathologie du travail" and "L'Organisation du travail contre l'unité du travailleur" in *Les histoires de la psychologie du travail*, ed. Y. Clot (Paris: Octares, 1996).